India:
Bilateral and Regional Economic Co-operation

India:
Bilateral and Regional Economic Co-operation

By

Gautam Murthy
Professor of Economics,
Centre for Indian Ocean Studies,
Osmania University, Hyderabad

New Century Publications
New Delhi, India

NEW CENTURY PUBLICATIONS
4800/24, Bharat Ram Road,
Ansari Road, Daryaganj,
New Delhi - 110 002 (India)

Tel.: 011-2324 7798, 4358 7398, 6539 6605
Fax: 011-4101 7798
E-mail: indiatax@vsnl.com • info@newcenturypublications.com
www.newcenturypublications.com

Editorial office:
LG–7, Aakarshan Bhawan,
4754-57/23, Ansari Road, Daryaganj,
New Delhi – 110 002

Tel.: 011-4356 0919

First Published: **2015**

ISBN: **978-81-7708-402-3**

Published by New Century Publications and printed at Salasar Imaging Systems, New Delhi.

Designs: Patch Creative Unit, New Delhi.

PRINTED IN INDIA

For my Dear Mother

Mrs. Rukmini Murthy

who imbibed in me the love of reading and writing, and who continues to inspire me in all my academic endeavours.

FOREWORD

This volume titled *India: Bilateral and Regional Economic Co-operation* by Professor Gautam Murthy captures the evolution of India's trade and economic relations with other countries/trade blocks.

The process of opening up of the Indian economy has given birth to a host of new challenges and opportunities. The spirit of the liberalisation process entails a conscious effort on the part of the policy makers to optimise on these opportunities-challenges trade-offs. When a definitive history of the reform process pursued in the Indian economy will be written, it would probably hinge on the synergy between the domestic and external sectors, each throwing up its strengths and threats.

The distinct improvement in the external sector in India has enabled a progressive liberalisation of the exchange and payments regime. The exchange rate is market-determined. Exchange rate management is flexible without fixed or pre-announced targets or bands, with interventions primarily to ensure orderly market conditions. India's exchange rate policy is perceived to be realistic and the exchange rate is among the least volatile in emerging market economies.

Against this backdrop, the greatest challenge facing the Indian economy is to enhance its productivity and competitiveness so as to achieve a sustained growth in exports of goods and services. Growth prospects can be enhanced considerably by tapping the opportunities offered by the international economy in terms of markets, investment and technologies along with improvement in efficiency and absorbing excess capacity available in the economy.

I have known Dr. Gautam Murthy for the past 40 years, both personally and professionally. I am quite familiar with his academic writings, and his views on international trade issues.

He has researched and published extensively on issues related to India's bilateral relations in general, and regional economic co-operation in particular. His scholarship and analytical skills are evident in the present collection of research papers.

Professor Murthy has provided useful insights into the emerging vistas of India's foreign economic policy. He has shown considerable pragmatism in his writings, which I am sure, would be found useful by both academicians and policy makers.

Dr. Biswajit Dhar

Director General,
Research and Information System for
Developing Countries (RIS),
New Delhi
May 1, 2014

About the Book

Prior to economic reforms process initiated in 1991, India had adopted a very cautious and guarded approach to regional economic co-operation with countries in the neighbourhood. Recognising that regional economic co-operation would continue to feature prominently in world trade, India engaged with its trading partners/blocks with the intention of expanding its export market and began concluding regional trade agreements (RTAs). Framework agreements have already been entered into with a number of trading partners with specific road maps to be followed and specified time frames by which the negotiations are to be completed.

India unveiled the *Look East* policy in 1991. East Asia—including Japan, China, South Korea and ASEAN—is today India's largest trading partner, ahead of European Union (EU) and the US. Proliferation of Free Trade Agreements (FTAs) is the clearest evidence of Asian countries' desire to forge closer economic relationships.

RTAs in the world are characterized as the *spaghetti bowl* in which trade criss-crosses in a complex fashion between countries based on tariff differentials and complicated rules of origin. In recent years, India too is a part of many regional and bilateral groupings.

Since early 1990s, world economies have witnessed a paradigm shift towards market-oriented economic policies and a careful dismantling of obstacles in international trade. This has helped the smaller, emerging economies gain access to world markets, modern technologies and collaborations. This has also given them a window to the developed world and helped them understand the significant role of globalization as an instrument, which could be utilised not just to achieve economic efficiency, but also to eradicate poverty.

This book is a timely addition to the existing body of literature on India's economic and trade relations with different countries of the world.

About the Author

Dr. Gautam Murthy is Professor of Economics at the Centre for Indian Ocean Studies, Osmania University, Hyderabad. He did his Ph.D. on "Trade and Export Instability in the ASEAN Economies" from the Gokhale Institute of Politics and Economics, Poona University. He was also Professor at XLRI, Jamshedpur. He has more than 30 years of teaching and research experience. His published books include *International Trade and Economic Co-operation; Regionalism in the Indian Ocean Rim*; *Strengthening Indo-South African Relations*; *Trade and Economic Co-operation* and *International Economic Relations*. He has published more than 70 articles in leading journals.

He has participated in many international conferences, and delivered lectures at leading academic institutes in Austria, Czech Republic, Germany, Malaysia, Singapore, Switzerland, Thailand and Vietnam.

Contents

Preface

Bilateral and regional economic co-operation is an integral part of India's foreign trade policy, complementing the multilateral trading system. Prior to economic reforms process initiated in 1991, India had adopted a very cautious and guarded approach to regionalism. Recognising that regional economic co-operation would continue to feature prominently in world trade, India engaged with its trading partners/blocks with the intention of expanding its export market and began concluding in principle agreements and moving in some cases even towards comprehensive economic cooperation agreements (CECAs) which cover free trade agreements (FTAs) in goods, services, investments and identified areas of economic cooperation.

Framework agreements have already been entered into with a number of trading partners with specific road maps to be followed and specified time frames by which the negotiations are to be completed. Joint study groups have also been set up for examining feasibility of CEÇAs between India-Japan, India-Brazil-South Africa and India-Russia. India and European Commission have also set up a High Level Trade Group (HLTG) as mandated by the India-EU Summit held in New Delhi on September 7, 2005. The mandate of the HLTG is to explore ways and means to increase bilateral economic flows including the possible launching of negotiations on a comprehensive trade and investment agreement.

India unveiled the *Look East* policy in 1991. East Asia—including Japan, China, South Korea and ASEAN—is today India's largest trading partner, ahead of EU and the US. Proliferation of free trade agreements (FTAs) is the clearest evidence of Asian countries' desire to forge closer economic relationships. The growing importance of CECA's indicates that such agreements are becoming deeper, extending to areas beyond just tariff reduction. Intra-regional trade and investment require building up of shared infrastructure. Many Asian countries have joined together to develop cross-border infrastructure to lay the foundations for closer trading relationships and increased connectivity among countries.

Asia remains one of the least integrated regions lacking a continent-wide regional organization. Forging closer links among Asian nations through appropriate institutional mechanisms can lead to substantial enhancement of national, regional and global productivity and output. In the past, India had adopted a very cautious approach to regionalism, and was engaged in only a few bilateral/regional initiatives, mainly through preferential trade agreements (PTAs).

The proliferation of regional trade agreements (RTAs) in the world is characterized as the *spaghetti bowl* in which trade criss-crosses in a complex fashion between countries based on tariff differentials and complicated rules of origin. In recent years, India too is a part of many regional and bilateral groupings. While there are benefits from these RTAs for Indian exports, in some cases the benefits to the partner countries are much more, with net gains of incremental exports from India being small or negative.

WTO's creation in 1995 marked the biggest reform of international trade since 1948. During those 47 years, international commerce had come under GATT which helped establish a prosperous multilateral trading system. However, by the end of 1980s an overhaul was due.

The eighth round of multilateral trade negotiations held under GATT and lasting for seven years (1986-1993) named Uruguay Round, resulted in new legal agreements for trade and strengthening settlement system. Following this, there was a Ministerial conference in Marrakesh, Morocco in April 1994 attended by 125 government representatives from across the world to sign for the establishment of a new successor institution of GATT, namely the World Trade Organization (WTO). It is an embodiment of the Uruguay Round results. WTO entered into force on January 1, 1995, with all assets and liabilities of GATT transferred to the former. Geneva is its headquarters. WTO replaced General Agreement on Tariffs and Trade (GATT) which remained in existence from 1948 to 1994. GATT was a multilateral treaty, governing trade in goods only. WTO is much wider in scope and coverage.

Since early 1990s, world economies have witnessed a paradigm shift towards market-oriented economic policies and a careful dismantling of obstacles in international trade. This has helped the smaller, emerging economies gain access to world markets, modern technologies and collaborations. This has also given them a window to the developed world and helped them understand the significant role of globalization as an instrument, which could be utilised not just to achieve economic efficiency, but also eradicate poverty.

The issue that concerns developing countries is how one can ensure greater participation of the weaker economies in the global process and what needs to be done to ensure that the course of globalization benefits more people in more countries. The uneven and unequal nature of the present globalization is manifested in the fast growing gap between the rich and poor people of the world and between developed and developing countries and by the large differences among nations in the distribution of gains and losses.

Although the developed world is in a dominant position and has been prepared to use this to further their control of the global economy, the developing countries have not done well in organising themselves to co-ordinate on substantial policy and negotiating positions. The developed countries, on the other hand, are well-organised within their own countries, with well-staffed departments dealing with international trade and finance, and with university academics and private and quasi-government think tanks helping to obtain information and map policies and strategies. They also have well-organised associations and lobbies associated with their corporations and financial institutions, which have great influence over the government departments.

Acknowledgements

I would like to place on record my deep appreciation for following scholars who have helped me over the years, both professionally and personally: Dr. Stephen P. Cohen, Senior Fellow, Foreign Policy Studies, Brookings Institution, Washington D.C.; Professor Hans-Liudger Diennel, Director, Berlin University of Technology and Nexus Institute for Co-operation Management and Interdisciplinary Research GmbH, Berlin; Dr. Charan D. Wadhva, President, Centre for Policy Research, New Delhi, and Fr. T.A Mathias, Dean, XLRI, Jamshedpur. My close friends in the Government of India, Mr. Ranjit Rae (Indian Foreign Service), and Mr. Rajan S. Katoch (Indian Administrative Service), gave me valuable academic advice on many occasions.

I sincerely thank my dear parents, brother, and wife for their constant support and encouragement over the years.

Hyderabad **Gautam Murthy**

1

South-South Cooperation

In view of the rigid posture of the North, the South should be prepared for a long struggle and its strength lies in collective action. The Group of 77 has decided to work in harmony and reconcile their differences instead of maintaining a façade of solidarity. However, as one UN slogan puts it "there is more to building bridges across the South, than drafting blueprints". Nearly all action and advances under the slogan of "collective self-reliance" and ECDC (Economic Cooperation among Developing Countries) have been only on the negotiating front. The organic linkage building has been largely peripheral. There are still only a few takers for India's proposal for a modest fund for technical feasibility studies on joint projects in the developing nations.

The response to proposals for a Third World Secretariat and a South-South Commission are at best lukewarm. An investment institution based on business like promises and untainted by concessionality does not elicit a very favourable response. Even the proposal for a finance facility, with capital from voluntary contributions in the form of grants and long-term loans from multilateral financial institutions is relegated for "further examination" by the Group of 77. Greater inter-developing country links will be smoother and the concept of collective self-reliance and mutual interdependence, which aims at expanding the degree of South-South cooperation will be pursued vigorously, san economic rivalries and intra-regional political power struggles.

The concept of ECDC first codified in Georgetown, Guyana, in 1972, was adopted by the Algiers Non-Aligned Summit of 1973. The specific action in a series of priority areas was decided at the fourth ministerial meeting of the

Group of 77 at Arusha, Tanzania, in February 1979. The action plan identified three priority areas: (i) a GSTP (Global System of Trade Preferences) among developing countries; (ii) cooperation among their state trading organizations (STOs), and (iii) the setting up of multinational marketing enterprises (MMEs). The framework of ECDC calls for rationalising intra-developing country trade, for bringing into tune, monetary and financial matters, for reforming institutions and re-directing and re-orienting policies where necessary. It means new international mechanisms and a multiplicity of linkages forged by developing countries themselves and woven into their national policy fabric.

The current flows of international trade indicate the low level of economic interdependence and integration of the markets of the developing economies, both for buying their importables and selling their exportables as well.

The commodities exported by the developing countries offered only limited opportunities for expansion of intra-regional exchanges in the past. The scope for trade was limited by a broad similarity of natural environment and in the absence of sufficient diversification of non-primary output, these economies contained only a very limited element of complementarity.

However, the bias of trade against developing countries is only a myth. The proximity, opportunities for intra-industry trade, and the importance of similar demand patterns, imply that developing countries ought to trade much more with one another. The strategy of import substitution for many smaller countries can become viable if all the developing countries come together, because in that case they would be able to reap dynamic economies of scale like unification of markets and the adoption of modern technology.

The NICs (Newly Industrializing Countries), chiefly Hong Kong, South Korea, Singapore, Taiwan, Mexico, Brazil and India can help the less industrializing developing countries. The product range exported by the NICs has diversified very dramatically. In recent years, goods requiring complex technologies, sophisticated skills, and large scale production have emerged as the fastest growing components of exports, though traditional labour intensive items still constitute the large bulk of inter-developing country exports. Some of these newly industrializing developing countries are even competing with established multinational companies in selling turnkey plants, consultancy services and other types of manufacturing know-how.

Production complementarities among developing countries have increased significantly in recent years, though still far short of the optimum. During the 1970s, their mutual trade grew faster than their trade with developed countries, and many had developed manufacturing interest, technologies and skills and diversified export capability. The simultaneous demand for raw materials by the NICs, and the quest for new markets for products in demand by developing countries, should create a vast trade potential among Third World countries.

Sub-regional and regional integration—a grouping among the developing countries—indicates that trade preferences stimulate mutual trade and steps up production. However, the benefits from joint action may be easy to demonstrate, but difficulties of effective implementation are also apparent.

Monetary and financial cooperation is a vital part of ECDC. Since the mid-1970s, there has been a great deal of Third World activity in the monetary and financial fields to promote production and trade through credit and clearing arrangements as well as to correct imbalances in the balance of payments and other distortions.

The horizontal South-South linkages could expect to diminish the effect of escalating prices of manufactured imports from the North. Even more important, they could expect to get from Third World countries, technology more appropriate to their conditions and needs. Intensified inter-developing country links in technology combined with a policy to promote appropriate products and techniques to restrict the import of inappropriate products and techniques could be an important way for developing countries to get away from dominance of North in technology sale.

Institutional machinery of the Third World must be revamped for effective ECDC, as the entire infrastructure of international trade is still owned and controlled by the North, which has maintained its dominance through control of financial and market mechanisms.

ECDC aims should include, on the one hand developing the South's own transportation capability, and on the other, getting the existing transport system to operate more advantageously to developing country needs. They involve Third World multinational transport facilities and services—road and rail—particularly for land-locked countries, as well as sea and exclusive liner containers and joint shipping services around and within regions. Third World cooperation is also needed to improve telecommunication networks as well as technology. The three crises of energy, food and population also have immense scope for developing country cooperation in R&D, sharing of technologies and techniques, distribution of investment and effort.

For example, in food, South-South cooperation could create the possibility of countries sharing the manufacturing component—one country producing fertilizers, another some other input, one making the manual aids, another heavier machinery, and the storage and buffer stocking, with a general interchange of training, research and information. It could develop new agricultural programmes in which cash surplus Southern countries invest in food production in other countries, which cannot afford the necessary inputs, and buy some of the surplus.

The more developed among the Southern countries can undertake a number of joint ventures in the less developed countries. Turnkey projects by engineering construction companies should be intensified. The investor-entrepreneurs of the NICs should play the role of "partners in development" at the instance of the host country and provide greater training facilities for their personnel. Hardcore technical expertise can be provided by member countries which have the experts and are willing to loan them. Exchange of expertise in consultancy and related services should prove most beneficial.

Cooperation and interchange of information among developing countries for the development of new and renewable sources of energy, chiefly, solar, mini and macro plants for hydroelectricity, wind, fuel and biogas, should be an integral part of South-South relations.

The finance facility should include infrastructural activity as well, such as transmission and distribution of power, roads and railways, shipping and airways.

Priority in the supply of exportable primary commodities and direct inter-government contact between exporting countries, and a common front in commodity negotiations, by agreeing to uniform quotas, should guide South-South understanding.

The trade of developing countries with one another is also more capital intensive than with industrialised countries as empirical evidence shows. Manufactured exports to industrialised countries are almost half as capital intensive as those to developing countries. Trade among developing countries in capital goods is beneficial for both exporters and importers. Capital goods amounted to 16 percent of trade among developing countries and only 55 of their trade with industrialised countries in 1977, as a World Bank study shows. In brief, South-South trade is thought to be better than North-South trade because of opportunities for learning by doing, the shared technological requirements of the South, and the advantages of appropriate technology embodied in capital goods produced by developing countries, and the exploitation of economies of scale.

ECDC must cause industrialisation, as widespread cooperation in various sectors progress. Industrial growth is largely a matter of opportunity and economies of scale. Product specialization and complementary industrial schemes, sharing know-how, natural and human resources, industrial design and promotion, cooperation in management of state enterprises and programmes free of big business shackles should be stepped up.

South-South cooperation not only offers scope for national development and bargaining power vis-à-vis North, but endless opportunity for innovation, for exploring areas in employment, job satisfaction and human relations in general, which have been uncharted and which are beyond the reach of the economically well established North.

Developing countries faced deteriorating terms of trade and a marked decline in the growth rate of world trade in real terms in 1980-81. Protectionist barriers are being raised by the industrialised countries and commercial credit at high interest rates are becoming the only source of external finance for developing countries. As Arthur Lewis says, "The South has within it most or all of the raw materials and energy supplies it might need, and ample land for food production". It is capable of saving the capital required for modernization. Also, the fallacy that there is no complementarity in the economies of LDCs still persists. The developing countries collectively have the requisite financial strength to set up their own equivalent of IMF and IBRD.

The vision and structure of collective self-reliance and economic cooperation among developing countries emerged out of necessity. But, having emerged this far, progress to implementation has been less than conspicuous. The fact that benefits from joint action, while easy to demonstrate, face difficulties of effective implementation. However, the realisation that collective action is imperative, if not indispensable, has now gathered momentum.

2

India's Look East Policy

Introduction

ASEAN today has ten members, covering all the countries of Southeast Asia from Myanmar in the extreme west to Vietnam in the extreme east. ASEAN has also emerged as a major force in international relations, with the ARF (ASEAN Regional Forum) given great importance by all great powers including China, the U.S., Russia and Japan. The high-profile EAS (East Asia Summits) consisting of ASEAN, China, India, Japan, South Korea, Australia and New Zealand and from 2011, U.S. and Russia, also draws worldwide attention.

India has moved purposefully in developing a broad economic and strategic partnership with these dynamic countries of Southeast Asia. In pursuance of India's "Look East" policy, the dialogue has moved consistently forward from a sectoral dialogue relationship in 1992 to membership of the high-profile strategic forum ARF (ASEAN Regional Forum) in 1996 and the Indo-ASEAN summits since 2002. In 2009, an Indo-ASEAN TIG (Trade in Goods) Agreement was signed. India's trade with ASEAN increased by 5.3 percent in 2011-2012, touching US$ 71.8 billion mark, and with such a rate of growth the target of US$ 100 billion by 2015 would be feasible. When ASEAN, China, Japan, and South Korea are included in the trade ambit of India, we gain strongly by more than US$ 150 billion annually. ASEAN in 2014 was India's fourth-largest trading partner, after the EU (European Union), US and China.

Indian Cultural Influences in Southeast Asia

When we refer to thousand year old ties, which unite Southeast Asia with India, it is not at all a hyperbole. In fact, it was about 2000 years ago, that the first navigators—Indian merchants—set foot in the region presently constituting the ASEAN nations.

India does not evoke the memories of an imperialist past in Southeast Asian minds. "Indian thought", Swami Vivekananda said "penetrated the world". Before Buddhism, Vedanta had penetrated into China, into Persia, and the islands of the Eastern Archipelago of Southeast Asia. The process of sustained contacts between indigenous people and alien cultures made Southeast Asia a politico-cultural fault zone characterized by transition and instability, on account of which the Southeast Asian region was described as the "Balkans of the East".

The people of Southeast Asia looked upon India as "a holy land rather than a motherland, a region of pilgrimage, rather than an area of jurisdiction". From Indianisation, was born a series of kingdoms based on the Hindu-Buddhist practices. Funan, Champa, Langkasuka (the first two centuries A.D.), Mon kingdoms of Thaton, Pegu and Pyu (before the beginning of the sixth century A.D.), Mataram (towards the ninth century A.D.), Chenla (seventh and eight centuries), Angkor (ninth and fifteenth centuries), Majapahit (fourteenth century), were Indianised states enjoying much pre-eminence and prestige.

Indian contacts did not end in the thirteenth and fifteenth centuries. Recent researchers in maritime history throw evidence of extensive Indian contact with Southeast Asia during the medieval period. But, it was not until the thirteenth century onwards that "Theravada Buddhism" and somewhat later Islam began to be propagated as popular religions that the external influences began to make an impact on the ordinary villager.

The Indian Muslims largely accomplished Islamisation in the archipelago region without resorting to force. The local rulers accepted the new faith in as much the same way as their ancestors had adopted Hinduism and Buddhism.

The historical edifices built during the reins of Indianised kingdoms like SriVijaya, Sailendra, Majapahit, the retention of

Indo-Sanskratic vocabulary, and the place names of Malaya, Java, Sumatra and alike, literary masterpieces based on Ramayana and the Mahabharata themes, living Indian traditions in the Bali islands and cherishing the names drawn from Indian mythology (like the Garuda Airlines of Indonesia, Sukarno, Megawati, Mahathir, Borneo—a corrupted form of Barun (Varun)—the Hindu God, are all the legacies of the glorious Indian cultural influences on the Malayo-Indonesian archipelago. It is an exciting experience of the visitors across Southeast Asia to come across such fascinating names of people, places, roads and national buildings, resembling those of Indian origin.

The Indian influence on Farther India (Southeast Asia) was all pervasive in the form of a magnificent cultural efflorescence, as evident from other aspects like polity, mythology, religion and philosophy, art and architecture, dance, drama, folklore, music, language, literature and farming methods. Apart from Indianised kingdoms that created a niche for themselves in the history of India and Southeast Asia, the architectural monuments like Angkor Vat, Pagan, and Borobudur are mute testimonies to the Indian cultural influence on art and architecture, language and other aspects.

Trade links between India and Southeast Asia were considerable and continuous. With them went all the wealth of India—thinking, philosophy, and art. Not only Buddhism, but Hinduism too became an indigenous religion, and great kingdoms and empires flourished. The state too became an indigenous religion, and great kingdoms and empires flourished. The State structures that developed were very similar. Art and architecture developed in tandem as if there were no sea barriers, with South India connected with some areas and East India with others. Sanskrit was so much the language of learning that Chinese waiters advised travellers to learn it in "Swarnadwipa"—the Indian name for Indonesia and Malaysia.

Asian history and culture is a complex fabric in which

many strands have become intertwined. Each culture is unique and rightly proud of what it has to contribute to the world. In the face of diversity and adversity in several respects, there is an underlying cultural unity binding the people of South and Southeast Asia. The Indian cultural legacy has been recognized and acknowledged. However, they are deeply sensitive to talk of "Greater India"—even if made as a casual comment. India should continue being a benign neighbour, playing a positive role in the economic, cultural, and political growth of the enlarged ten members of ASEAN.

Thus, India and the ASEAN states can work together, in the twenty-first century world, with their shared cultural values.

Territorial Ambit of Asia

Asia is essentially a geographical expression. It covers the Arabic-speaking countries in West Asia, Israel, Turkey and Iran, SAARC (including Afghanistan), Southeast Asia, and East Asia covering China, Japan and the Korean peninsula.

All the Asian countries comprise a variety of ethnic groups, languages and faiths. Historically there has been no evolution of an "Asian entity" or an "Asian identity". This is in marked contrast to the unifying embrace of a Latin American identity, which brings the people of South and Central America together, a Caribbean identity, an African identity, a North American identity and a European identity. This sense of shared identity has already found institutional expression in the European Union, the Organization of American States, or the African Union (AU). In contrast, in Asia there are at least three large groupings—the Arabic-speaking countries of West Asia, SAARC and the ASEAN. The remaining countries remain territorially unaffiliated. The UN (United Nations) however divides Asia between its Arabic-speaking members in the Economic Commission for West Asia and all other Asian countries into ESCAP, which brings together the Asian countries with countries of the Pacific as well—ranging from Australia and New Zealand to diverse island countries of the

Pacific like Togo and Vanuatu. It is only in the last few years of the last century and more so in the present century that one talks of a unified, 'Asian Century'.

The idea of Asia has also expanded so as now to include the Central Asian Republics of the former Soviet Union. However, when one talks of an 'Asian Century', we only include member states of ASEAN, China, Japan, Republic of Korea and India. West Asia, Central Eurasian countries (former Soviet Republics) and remaining member countries of SAARC are ignored.

Asia is a region of multiple heterogeneities –geographic, economic, political and social. The region does not lack natural and human resources, but lacks initiatives for building complementarities. A closing of the ranks in the whole of Asia will ensure greater reciprocity in economic relations with Europe and North America. Often, it is argued that the size and dynamism of the Asian economy is a potentially autonomous engine of growth, which need not exclusively depend on the health and policy imperatives of developed countries of Europe and North America. The Asian region as a whole accounts today for 50 percent of global exports, 40 percent of global imports, and 60 percent of global international reserves.

A dynamic Asian economy could compensate to a substantial degree for the sluggish growth elsewhere. This growth potential derives from the large and diversified natural resource base and productive structures in the region. Its member countries produce everything from energy, vital minerals, tropical products, fibres and cereals. It covers industrial and trading capacities ranging from the most capital-intensive to the most labour-intensive, with a large and varied work force commanding different compensation levels. All these factors are highly conducive to a greater economic interaction. Some strategic observers have even noted that it may be desirable to take even Pakistan on board in a future Asian alliance. Thus, one could envisage a new Asian economic and strategic architecture including the East Asia

Summit members SCO (Shanghai Cooperation Organization) members, as well as all other South, West and Central Eurasian countries.

India and ASEAN: Geo-political Realities

India gradually began to get disillusioned with Asia, as the U.S. began to isolate India with regional pacts like CENTO and SEATO. The Chinese also began to get overassertive, and India's complete disillusionment of playing a greater role in Asia, came with the Sino-Indian war of 1962. The Pakistan aggression of 1965, also made India turn away from her immediate neighbourhood. India at the same time began forging close ties both politically and economically with the Soviet Union. It must be admitted that the Soviet Union played a stellar role in shaping India's infrastructure, by helping India build her steel plants and large irrigation dams (which Nehru called the "Temples of Modern India"), the benefits of which India is reaping even today. Also, the Soviet Union helped India politically and in the defence sphere, and was a timely ally in India's moments of crisis. The defence relationship continues even today, with more than 75 percent of our defence equipment still coming from Russia. Modern Russia—a mineral, petroleum and gas rich superpower—will continue to be in India's strategic focus, despite India's diplomatic closeness with the United States, after the Indo-US Nuclear Agreement.

India's geo-political and more so geo-economic compulsions of allying with the FSU (Former Soviet Union), and away from Asia in the 1960s and 1970s must thus be viewed in its totality. Such was Nehru's disillusionment with Asia, that when Tunku Abdul Rahman, the former Prime Minister of Malaysia, and Lee Kuan Yew, the former Prime Minister of Singapore, approached him with the idea of forming an economic alliance with Southeast Asia, he tersely told them, "I have nothing to do with the Cocoa Cola economies". Prime Minister Indira Gandhi, also assiduously forged ties with the Indo-Chinese States, particularly Vietnam in the Cold War days. Support for India's association with the expanded ASEAN region is readily forthcoming because of Indira Gandhi's initiatives in the 1970s and 1980s. Rajiv Gandhi also played a role in renewing ties with Asia, with his path-breaking visit to China in 1988. His handshake with the legendary Chinese leader Deng Xiao Ping, set of a chain-reaction in restructuring Sino-Indian and India-Asia relations.

India initially perceived the establishment of ASEAN as an extension of the American sphere of influence. It viewed the origin of ASEAN as being political in its nature using regional economic co-operation merely as a rational for justifying its existence. The ASEAN countries viewed India as a satellite of the former Soviet Union. India's pro-Soviet line of handling its foreign policy on Vietnam and Cambodia in the 1970s and 1980s irked most of the ASEAN countries, and added to the political distance between India and ASEAN.

ASEAN-India Economic Dimensions

India's relatively closed economy before 1990 also did not provoke interest among ASEAN, which had changed their strategies since the early 1970s towards outward-looking and more open economies. Lee Kuan Yew even advised Indira Gandhi "you may be non-aligned, but align yourself with the international market grid, and gate crash into the free market".

With the collapse of the Berlin Wall in 1989, and the disintegration of the Soviet Union soon after, the political freeze in relations between India and ASEAN made no sense. The improvement of India's relations with China since the mid-1980s, also improved the political environment in the ASEAN countries for strengthening economic co-operation with India. India's post-1991 economic reforms transformed the Indian economy to an attractive destination for expanding and diversifying the market for ASEAN exports. This has been very nicely put by Thomas Friedman in his book, "The World is flat", in the chapter "When the Walls Came Down, and the

Windows Went Up".

The ASEAN countries also discovered several new complementarities among their economies, and the Indian economy. The surplus capital of some of the ASEAN countries could be put to good economic use by combining it with the globally recognized skills of scientific, technical, professional, and managerial manpower of India. India's defence capabilities, non-aggressive historical record and commitment to maintenance of peace in the world and in Asia are recognized. The combined effect of the fundamentally altered economic, political and strategic environment in the ASEAN region, led the ASEAN grouping to clearly recognize the mutual benefits of strengthening economic relations with India.

The foundations of India's "Look East" policy were laid by Prime Minister P.V. Narasimha Rao. His famous Singapore lecture of 1994 in which he announced India's intention to use the Asia-Pacific region "as a spring board for India's leap into the global marketplace" ushered in India's new engagement with Asia. The "Look East" initiatives are now pursued with renewed vigour, and today what we need is a "Focus East" policy. Today, India's "gaze" towards ASEAN is so strong, that China and the United States are beginning to get wary of us.

The next step for India is to look beyond the ASEAN-East Asian region, and extend the policy to the vast Asia-Pacific region. It should also cover besides economic, strategic and socio-cultural issues as well. There is much scope for further expanding and deepening our co-operative agenda, synergizing the economies of India and the ASEAN and exploring new avenues for diplomatic complementarities.

India-ASEAN co-operation has progressed substantially in many spheres-mainly in science and technology, tourism, trade and investment. The level of investment flows on both sides also has progressed substantially, but still has a lot of untapped potential.

Geo-economics of Indo-ASEAN Engagement

The relevance of geo-economic relations as the dominant

force in shaping the future of international and regional relations is most likely to grow substantially in the 21st century—notwithstanding the expanding role of WTO. In this noticeably altered global and regional context, economic diplomacy will increasingly overshadow the traditional political and geo-strategic dimensions of the foreign policy formulations of the decades to come. A coalitional approach to the management of power relations at the regional levels is most likely to be preferred in the economic sphere. The future battles arising from conflicts of national interests are most likely to be fought in the global/regional markets, rather than on battlefields.

While small-scale or domestic conflicts are undermining peace and security of almost every sub-region in the Indian Ocean, large-scale regional security and strategic matters are also gaining in primacy, including the rise of terrorism. The large foreign military presence, the proliferation of weapons of mass destruction and missile capabilities, the security of sea lanes of communications (SLOCs), as well as smuggling and piracy at sea are getting increasing attention. In the pacific resolution of domestic conflicts, negotiation takes place in specific case-by-case forums, rather than in large multilateral region-wide organizations. Some Indian oceanic multilateral commitments on peace and security issues could certainly help to limit conflict escalation and their negative impact at the sub-regional scale.

Within its three specific protocols, and its regional forum, the ASEAN Regional Forum (ARF) addressing peace, security and stability issues, ASEAN has developed an original framework that could certainly serve as a model for the development of a formal Indian oceanic co-operation on these matters.

It is thus obvious that regional co-operation in peace, security, and strategic matters could help limit ongoing conflict situations, prevent new conflicts, promote disarmament and non-proliferation, and address the role of foreign militaries in the region, thus generating a more stable geo-political environment. India has recently consciously attempted to provide explicit economic orientation to its foreign policy—the "“Look East” policy for consciously expanding its economic linkages with ASEAN countries.

India's key position at the head of the Indian Ocean, astride the East-West trade route is an asset. Today, India's strategic influence stretches to both the entry points to the Indian Ocean—from the Straits to the Indian Ocean; from the Straits of Hormuz in the West, to the Straits of Mallaca in the East. The bulk of India's foreign trade is seaborne; besides protecting its long coastline and SLOCs, it has to adequately patrol her 200 kilometres EEZ (exclusive economic zone), where there is frequent poaching by modern and fast Southeast Asian vessels. Threats from Pakistan and more recently the growing menace of the Chinese Navy, which has started making its presence felt in the Indian Ocean region through the Coco islands in the North Andamans Sea, are increasing.

India considers the Indian Ocean region well within its sphere of influence—and thus trade with the Southeast Asian countries, now all part of the ASEAN—assumes added importance in the emerging geo-economic strategies of India. Indo-ASEAN co-operation can serve as a stabilising factor in promoting India's geo-strategic interests in the Indian Ocean region.

ASEAN-India Co-operation in Emerging Area

There is much scope for further expanding and deepening our co-operative agenda, synergising the economies of India and ASEAN and exploring new avenues for diplomatic complementarities. India-ASEAN cooperation has progressed substantially in many spheres, mainly in science and technology, IT and electronics, HRD, transport and infrastructure, space technology, tourism and trade and investment. These initiatives are however not adequately reflected in trade figures.

The level of investment flows on both sides has a lot of untapped potential and can easily rise to a great extent with sustained efforts by both sides. The redeeming fact is that there are substantial investments by both India and ASEAN in each other's countries.

Although there have been significant changes in commodity composition of India's trade with ASEAN countries in recent years, components of the trade basket could do with substantial revision, with an increasing emphasis on India moving up the value chain.

India should also intensify its marketing thrust to ASEAN countries to correct the asymmetry in trade relations. Both infrastructure and technology can be hawked much more aggressively. Our exporters should negotiate much harder, offer more competitive terms, adhere to delivery schedules, and provide effective after-sales service. A marketing culture among our exporters, combined with a bit of hard sell, could help India make decisive inroads into the ASEAN markets.

Intensive efforts to promote business synergies on the two sides in areas such as infrastructure, IT, biotechnology, and tourism got a positive boost with the India-ASEAN Business Summits. A trade pact with ASEAN is the best beginning since India has traditionally enjoyed many links—economic and strategic—with the region, although there is a lot of untapped potential. We should also try to strengthen strategic alliances with the *guanxi* (overseas Chinese networks) who control most of the distribution channels in Malaysia, Singapore and to some extent in Thailand.

India should also make available information on its capabilities in fields like IT, and market these better in countries like the Philippines and Brunei, as trade with these two ASEAN countries is virtually non-existent.

The terms of India-ASEAN engagement needs to be taken much more seriously. The possibilities for functional co-operation are limitless, and enthusiasm should translate into tangible gains. Tourism, culture and education are given precedence and priority in the co-operative framework. Transport, communications and infrastructure will be prioritised in the next phase. The MGC also provides immense opportunities for India's private sector to create a niche in the region; India can make up for its past mistakes. Indo-ASEAN cooperation in tourism, culture and education can also be strengthened in Indonesia and Malaysia.

It must be remembered that India's cultural footprints in Southeast Asia have been left because of trade and religion, and not because of show of power.

India's relations with ASEAN assume significance also in the light of the various cultural similarities it shares with the region. Buddhism is the natural link to Southeast Asia, particularly the Mekong basin. The cultural ties with Southeast Asia need to be stressed apart from trade and Buddhism.

ASEAN can also source its manpower requirements—technical and managerial—from India, as manpower here is both competitive and culturally compatible. Indian professionals teaching English and computer skills can raise the standards of education and knowledge base. The ASEAN-India HRD programme needs to be further strengthened.

References

Ali, Alatas, "Clash of Civilizations? No it is Pure Evil", *Straits Times*, 16th July, 2004.

"Asian Economic Integration: Vision of a New Asia", Conference Proceedings, RIS, Tokyo, November 2004.

Bajpai, Kanti, "Enhancing Ties between India and Southeast Asia: An Indian View", in India, Southeast Asia and the United States: New Opportunities and Prospects for Co-operation, Satu P. Limaye and Ahmed Mukarram (eds.), ISEAS, Singapore, 1998.

Bedi, Rahul, "A New Doctrine for the Indian Navy", *Frontline,* July 2004.

Cohen, Roger, "The Roar of a New Asia is in the Global Horizon", *International Herald Tribune,* April 2005.

Devare, Sudhir, "India and Southeast Asia: Towards Security Convergence, ISEAS, Singapore and Capital Publishing company, New Delhi, 2006.

Frank, Jurgen Richter and Pamela C., "Recreating Asia: Visions for a New Century", John Wiley and Sons, 2002.

Friedman, Thomas, "The World is Flat", Allen Pane, Penguin Books,

2005.
Gare, Frederic and Amitabh Mattoo (eds.), "India and ASEAN: The Politics of India's Look East Policy", Manohar Publishers, New Delhi, 2001.
Gonsalves, Eric (ed.), "Asian Relations", India International Centre, Lancer International, 1991.
Osius, Ted and Raja C. Mohan, "Enhancing India-ASEAN Connectivity", Centre for Strategic and International Studies, Washington, D.C., 2013.
Nagarajan, S., "Buddhism in Southeast Asia", Report of the Centre for Studies on Indo-China and South Pacific, Tirupati, 1998.
Panchamukhi, V.R. and Rehman Sobhan (eds.), "Towards an Asian Economic Area", Macmillan, New Delhi, 1995.
Reddy, Yagama, "The Saga of Indian Culture in Southeast Asia: Retrospect and Prospect", Report of the Centre for Studies on Indo-China and South Pacific, Tirupati, 1998.
Weatherbee, Donald E., "International Relations in Southeast Asia: The Struggle for Autonomy", Rowman and Littlefield Publishers, London, 2009.

3

India and Association of Southeast Asian Nations (ASEAN)

Relevance of Regional Groupings

The Indian Ocean region has a spectrum of ocean activities, like harnessing fishery resources, extraction of drugs from the sea, offshore mining, coastal zone management, protection of ports and harbours, production of offshore oil and gas, and extraction of energy from the sea, which needs to be safeguarded. This expanding spectrum of ocean activities has brought in additional tension spots such as demarcating maritime boundaries, rivalry for seabed exploitation, island grabbing, smuggling, poaching, terrorism at sea and safety of offshore platforms. The other flash points are the movement by sea, of narcotics, weapons, chemicals and fissionable material. This has led to fresh norms, conventions and rules encompassing the legal regime of the seas, naval arms control, safety of ship and seafarers and traffic separation in international choke points. Hence, peace in the region is of paramount importance, and should be pursued sincerely. One of the effective measures for ensuring peace is regional cooperation. Regional cooperation among the various sub-regions of the larger Indian Ocean region can be effective in exploiting regional complementarities and economies of scale. Besides the pure economic aspects of cooperation, regional cooperation by bringing about diplomatic cohesion and by reducing regional tensions can be effective in keeping out negative extra-regional influences.

The Indian Ocean region, comprising littoral and hinterland countries, where the waters of the Indian Ocean are taken as a link, is a region of growing geo-strategic and economic significance in the global scenario. Despite the growing interrelationships among the Atlantic Ocean countries, and the emergence of the Pacific Ocean Rim countries as dynamic economies with growing international clout, the Indian Ocean will emerge even stronger as a focal point for international diplomatic and economic interests. The Indian Ocean region is a community of 40 sovereign countries with over one billion people. The people of the region have diverse cultural expressions, living in widely varied environments who are nevertheless linked through the complex webs of history, politics, economics and the environment. The waters of the Indian Ocean serve as a binding force, holding the vast area together.

The core of the "third world" is in the Indian Ocean region, and all the countries are in the U.N. category of "developing economies", with the exception of Australia. The region has both the NICs (Newly Industrializing Countries) of Asia and leading members of the Gulf/West Asia of OPEC (Organization of Petroleum Exporting Countries), and thus has enormous economic leverage in the world. From a strategic point of view, with big-power détente and demilitarization in the region, medium powers like India, Indonesia and Australia will play a more assertive role in safeguarding their own as well as the region's maritime interests. From an environment perspective also, the Indian Ocean region is of paramount importance, with protection of the rare flora and fauna of the region, safeguarding the rain forests with their complex bio-spherical relationships, pollution, overpopulation, deep sea fishing and exclusive zones, and a host of other issues interlinking environment and development demanding international attention. There are also fresh challenges in coping with the new global order, adjusting to decolonisation, and the social and economic forces generated by industrialisation and modernisation in the countries of the Indian Ocean region.

The Indian Ocean is the third largest ocean in the world, with about 40 percent of the global population residing in the region. The region is the poorest in the world, with the counties of both sub-Saharan Africa and the Indian sub-continent located here. Although the region is rich in raw materials and petroleum, the countries in it are still very much dependent on the industrialised countries of other regions.

The Indian Ocean region has five main sub-regions, namely Southern and Eastern Africa; Persian Gulf and the Horn of Africa; South Asia; Southeast Asia and Australia. It has four significant regional economic organisations, namely ASEAN, SAARC, SADCC and GCC. The SADCC (Southern African Development Coordination Conference) is an association of the nine States of the Southern African region. Members are Angola, Botswana, Lesotho, Malawi, Mozambique, Swaziland, Tanzania, Zambia and Zimbabwe. SADCC was formalised by the Lusaka Declaration of States and governments on April 1, 1980. The GCC (Gulf Cooperation Council) was established in May 1981 by six Arab States—Bahrain, Kuwait, Oman, Qatar, Saudi Arabia and the UAE (United Arab Emirates). The other two regional economic organisations, SAARC and ASEAN, are located in South and Southeast Asia respectively.

Regional cooperation within and between sub-regions in the larger Indian Ocean region can serve as an effective counter balance to the protectionist and insular trends among the developed countries of the other regions in the Northern Hemisphere. Regional cooperation can take the form of technology transfer, sharing managerial expertise, joint production and marketing facilities, besides pure commodity trade. Such synergetic networking among countries of the region can be effective in exploiting regional complementarities, by bringing about effective diplomatic cohesion; can keep out negative extra-regional influences.

In order to safeguard the interests of the countries of the third world in an increasingly competitive international system, regional cooperation is seen as a more fruitful way of tackling the problems of economic development and increasing the bargaining power of developing countries vis-à-vis the developed world. It serves as an effective way of reducing the dependence of the industrialised North.

The third world Sates, given their colonial legacy, lay greater stress on relations with advanced capitalist States through the North-South dialogue rather than on development through regional cooperation. In fact "regionalism" in the third world grew out of regional security or military-oriented organisations CENTO (Central Treaty Organisation) and SEATO (Southeast Asia Treaty Organisation)—formed with support from countries external to the region like the U.S. and U.K. From these security-oriented regional organisations in the 1950s to the economy-oriented organisations in the 1960s and beyond, the third world has shown greater assertiveness and independent thinking. Economic integration among LDCs (less developed countries) started after the late 1950s, encouraged by the success of unions in Europe, like the EEC (European Economic Community), EFTA (European Free Trade Area) and CMEA (Council for Mutual Economic Assistance).

Origins of ASEAN

Ad hoc measures and steps had been taken by countries of Southeast Asia, but it was not until 1967 that the five countries of the region—Indonesia, Malaysia, Philippines, Singapore and Thailand—joined together to form ASEAN (Association of Southeast Asian Nations). Brunei Darussalam joined in 1984. At the first ASEAN summit in Bali in1976, nine years after the formation of the group, the "Declaration of ASEAN Concord" was issued, setting before it a programme of action on the economic front. The mainstay of intra-ASEAN trade involves Singapore, Indonesia and Malaysia. Hence, the immediate impact of any bilateral trade concessions would not be substantial so long as the Philippines and Thailand are left out. The major instrument for the expansion of intra-regional trade continues to be the preferential trading arrangements (PTAs). The meeting of ASEAN economic ministers agreed on across-the-board 20 to 25 percent tariff cuts on the basis of value of trade in place of the earlier practice under PTA of offering products on an item-by-item, country-by-country basis.

Cooperation in Industry

Cooperation in industrial development was being sought through two main programmes, the AIP (ASEAN Industrial Project Scheme) and the AIC (ASEAN Industrial Complementation Programme). The main thrust of the AIP is government-to-government industrial collaboration projects, with the products of these undertakings to be accorded preferential access by the member countries. Five projects were to be established as joint ventures, with all member countries participating in the equity and sharing in the profits and risks. The equity investment will be shared among member countries at a ratio of 60 percent for the host country, and 10 percent for the other four members.

Under the AIC programme, entire industries can be developed on an ASEAN-wide basis. Specific industries are identified for complementary development in the private sector on a sub-regional basis and preferential tariff is to be accorded to their products. Two specific packages in the field of automotive products have been approved, with 50 percent preferential tariff margin. Other arrangements for industrial development by joint ventures among ASEAN private investors would also qualify for a 50 percent tariff reduction when traded between participating ASEAN countries.

AIJVs (ASEAN Industrial Joint Ventures), which are private sector equivalents of AIPs enjoy exclusivity and tariff preferences similar to AIC products. An AIJV requires only two participant countries instead of five; conceptual changes are being proposed to give AIJVs greater flexibility and increase their attractiveness to the private sector.

Cooperation is taking place in other fields as well. The ASEAN-CCI (Chambers of Commerce and Industry) has brought together business and industrialists of the member countries. It has also helped promote awareness of the necessity for deeper intra-ASEAN regional industrial investment. Intra-ASEAN contact in the banking, financial and professional fields have also been expanding.

Other sectors of importance for cooperation within the region are transportation and communications. Sea freight among the countries within the region is often costlier than outside the region. Telecommunications systems are, likewise, often more conveniently arranged with countries outside, than with neighbouring countries. Recognising the importance of food security on a regional basis for the people of the ASEAN sub-region, the AFSR (ASEAN Food Security Reserve) has been instituted.

Intra-regional Cooperation

Intra-regional economic cooperation is the most effective strategy to reduce ASEAN's heavy dependence on Japan and the industrialised West. ASEAN has achieved success in breaking the "psychological barrier" to regional cooperation; although greater subordination of national, political, and economic needs to the greater regional framework will no doubt take time.

Despite the apparent complementarity of ASEAN, like the same preferences for free-market economics with modest State intervention, there is a concealed competitiveness. All the member countries, except Singapore, depend on selling primary products to the developed world; and all six are developing industries geared to their domestic market, or to export to the developed world. Their levels of economic and social development also vary widely. The per capita incomes of Brunei, Singapore and Malaysia, for example, are more than fifteen, ten, and five times that of Indonesia respectively.

The ASEAN countries require large-scale investments of capital, technology and skills over a long period for modernisation, and to broaden their economic bases and choices. While some amount of intermediate goods, capital, technology and skill will be made available indigenously, the bulk of it will have to come from the West and Japan. This may dampen regional cooperation, and inject an additional element of competitiveness.

The policy of import substitution together with the balance of payments difficulties of some ASEAN countries have resulted in certain policies biased against regional trade. Thus, intra-regional trade of manufactured goods is almost negligible.

Benefits of Integration

Some economists still subscribe to the view that the first task at hand is economic development on a national scale; that the establishment of economically integrated sub-regions will in fact be hastened by concentrating first on national economic development, thereby enlisting the strong political forces of nationalism. But while each country has to develop according to its own development priorities and national resource endowments, both human and material, it is an accepted premise of development planning as well as proven from historical experience of both developed and developing countries, that the gains from trade as a result of regional cooperation far outweigh the advantages of autarkic development.

The European Economic Community (EEC), which first started as cooperation in only two sectors, steel and coal, among six member countries, was renamed European Community in 1993 and after the Treaty of Lisbon in 2009, was abolished and replaced by the European Union (EU). The tendency towards greater "economic fusion" in Europe is a result of the realisation that by coming together and sharing the benefits of economic specialisation, greater economies of scale and production complementarities can be achieved. Countries of the world are interdependent, and no country can achieve maximum potential unless it cooperates with other countries of the region.

Developing countries, by concentrating on development within and minimum trading with other countries, have achieved far less growth, than countries with greater export orientation, or which were part of regional economic groupings. Countries, which were part of EAC in Africa or the CARICOM in the Caribbean, have achieved higher growth rates than non-regional members. South Korea and Singapore, who have the highest export-to-GNP ratios not only in Asia, but also among the highest in the world, have also the highest overall growth rates, with very high social indicators as well.

Thus, there is no alternative to countries coming together in regional groupings to exploit regional complementarities and achieve a better bargaining position vis-à-vis non-regional members. Nationalism in the economic sense has given way to cooperative supra-nationalism, where the benefits far outweigh insular development. At the same time, we should realise that because of the common colonising legacy of the EEC countries, supra-nationalism is easier to achieve there than in ASEAN or SAARC, where colonialism has left bitter animosities and mutual antagonisms. Nevertheless, regional cooperation is the only way to defuse problems "left over from history", and promote beneficial economic interaction.

Given the limited size of ASEAN market, it is doubtful that a narrow regional approach to trade expansion could substitute for multilateral trade expansion. Relatively few manufactures, which are not competitive on the scale of output allowed by the market of a single ASEAN member, could be produced competitively for the ASEAN regional market. Thus, extensive economic cooperation with other regional organisations of Asia is imperative.

The SAARC countries of South Asia are also Asian developing countries, though they may be at much lower levels of economic and industrial development. Some of the commodities exported by SAARC countries—like tropical products and minerals—are of export interests to ASEAN as well. Thus, there exists vast scope for exploiting regional complementarities in the two sub-regions of the Indian Ocean region. We now give a background of attempts at regional co-operation in South Asia.

ASEAN and India

In economic and strategic terms, India wants to develop its North East by increasing its connectivity with the rest of the world through commercial linkages with ASEAN. By taking advantage of Myanmar's links with other ASEAN countries, India hopes to transform the North East from a *security burden* into a *land of economic opportunity*.

The Mekong basin also has the potential to emerge as a major granary as its vast lands are very fertile. India and Thailand can do much to tame the Mekong River, and enhance cultivation by spreading irrigation.

ASEAN also faces the problem of disparity in development, the new entrants—Laos, Vietnam and Cambodia showing lower levels of performance compared to the other members—and will take time to integrate fully into the ASEAN framework. India can offer its help here as well by providing interest-free credit facilities for speedier development of these countries, and cashing in on the tremendous goodwill that existed for her in the Cold War days.

There is also immense scope for further enhancing joint ventures in manufacturing, consultancy, leasing and trading outfits between India and ASEAN. The Indian bureaucracy is continuing to give explicit economic orientation to foreign policy. At the geo-political level, India's membership of the ARF (ASEAN Regional Forum), discussing security issues, can serve to effectively protect and project India's strategic interests in the region. While India's membership of ARF enables it to participate in regional security issues, we would seriously undermine our long-term strategic and economic interests, if we do not take into account China's rapidly expanding economic and strategic profile in our eastern neighbourhood.

India today has more intensive security links with America's allies in the ARF (Asian Regional Forum of ASEAN)—Australia, South Korea and Japan. India's improved ties with the U.S. have also created the space for a more confident and constructive engagement with China in both strategic and economic terms. India's new found enthusiasm to forge a trade pact with ASEAN also stands in stark contrast with its attitude towards SAARC, and even towards bilateral relations with its neighbours in South Asia. That a free trade area in South Asia remains a non-starter is not entirely the fault of Pakistan; India too has been reluctant to make the larger concessions that will make a more effective South Asian grouping. No country, particularly China should be allowed to dominate any future visions of an Asian Community, by practicing a "Monroe Doctrine for Asia", seeking absolute influence over the entire East Asian region.

ASEAN has a combined economy bigger than India or South Korea and a total population of over half a billion people. It has the potential to become an economic force that could rival China, India, Brazil and Russia. The absence of ASEAN from investors' radar screens as a unified economic unit is due to lack of integration of the bloc's economies and financial markets. Both local and international investors still widely view the Southeast Asian region as 10 separate economies due to differences in regulations, business environment, institutional capacity, and culture. Thus, further integration of ASEAN is necessary in order to maximize intra-regional synergies and keep the region relevant to the international economy and investors.

ASEAN has earned its way to the global high table. Its member countries have weathered the financial storm well. Economic activity did contract in some open economies such as Singapore, Thailand and Malaysia, but the worst is over, and their economies and financial systems have suffered no collateral damage. Indonesia and Vietnam are emerging as Asia's two outperformers. ASEAN's purchasing power could double by 2023, creating significant opportunities in consumer products and services.

ASEAN economies have built up their resilience through years of reforms and restructuring since the Asian financial crisis of 1997-98. The accumulation of foreign exchange reserves has helped maintain investor confidence and limit undue volatility while a well-capitalized banking sector has been critical to ensuring the smooth running of the region's economy. Indeed, the ASEAN region has all the ingredients to become a global economic force. As of August 2014, its 10 members had a combined GDP of US$ 2.3 trillion, 625 million people, and total trade of US$ 2.5 trillion in 2013. If ASEAN were a single-country, it would be the world's 10th largest economy, and the third most populous country. Counting only extra-regional trade, ASEAN is the world's fifth-largest trading power, after the US, Germany, China and Japan. In recent years ASEAN's free trade agreements with China, India, Japan, and South Korea have deepened the region's economic links with the rest of Asia.

ASEAN as a combined economy would rank among the world's top 10 in terms of FDI inflows. Fears of China taking every FDI dollar from ASEAN have not been matched by reality. ASEAN still managed to attract US$ 122 billion of FDI in 2013, with intra-regional investment accounting for a sizable portion as foreign investors, especially from within Asia, see countries such as Indonesia and Vietnam as alternative manufacturing bases as the cost of doing business in China rises. The region's economic integration is still at an early stage and much work is required to remove barriers to the trade of goods and the free flow of capital, information and talent. These measures are relevant to businesses as they enhance access to the whole ASEAN consumer market from any one member country.

Amid the rise of China and India, there are ongoing concerns that some of the Southeast Asian nations may be marginalised. This is primarily a result of the economic and political diversity of ASEAN members. For example, the World Bank's "Doing Business Survey, 2014" ranks Singapore as the easiest place in the world to do business, while it ranks Laos 159th out of 189 countries. Politically,

ASEAN's members range from Indonesia, the world's third largest democracy (after the U.S. and India), to Myanmar at the other end of the spectrum. Brunei's economy is heavily dependent on oil and gas. Thailand, Vietnam, Indonesia and Malaysia have considerable agricultural production bases. By contrast, Singapore has few, if any, natural resources, and relies on imports for local consumption and manufacturing; financial services and trading drives its economy.

Clearly, ASEAN's smaller members need a common platform to represent their interests and ASEAN could become that key channel through which these members can make their voices heard on the global stage. The challenge for ASEAN leaders at their fifteenth summit in Thailand was to convince the business sector and investors that ASEAN is a workable concept. The plan to establish an ASEAN Economic Community by 2015, while ambitious, is necessary to push the region's integration forward.

The FTA with ASEAN is an economic "win win" for both sides, although its merit lies more on its political and diplomatic impact on ASEAN. During negotiations lasting over six years when India dithered many times, an impression gathered in ASEAN countries that India was not serious about engaging Asia. Signing the FTA has signalled India's commitment to economic integration and political cooperation with Southeast Asia as a logical outcome of its "Look East Policy" (LEP).

The main thrust of our Southeast Asia policy being economic integration and energy security, LEP has less of a political, strategic or cultural dimension. Given India's effort to integrate with the global economy, diplomacy focuses more on trade and investment. India's LEP lacks a strategic vision of a future Asia-Pacific that can inform its policies and actions, helping it establish its rightful place in the Asian balance of power. Such failure to articulate a vision is pervasive of foreign policy in its entirety as India faces new challenges and opportunities in its rise to influence in an increasingly uncertain international environment. No major power's foreign policy can be effective without a guiding framework of underlying principles reflecting its geo-political requirements and values.

ASEAN looks towards India because of its potential as an economic powerhouse and partly to balance China's overwhelming economic and strategic influence. India should envisage a new strategic architecture for Asia and its own pivotal role in it. The recent global economic slowdown requires India to diversify its markets. It is imperative that India sends out strong positive signals and underline its commitment to be a partner in Asian growth and development.

India's LEP supported India's economic transformation and growth, expanded India's strategic space to pursue its national interests and pursue a proactive role in the ongoing process of Asian integration. Regional integration creates an "arc of prosperity", and is reflective of India's desire to see its neighbourhood transform into a "community".

India-ASEAN Cooperation in Tourism

National boundaries are today shrinking with the inter-linked effects of technology, information flows, foreign capital mobility and above all, the movement of people. With all these developments, and the image of India improving in the eyes of the world, the tourism scenario is also witnessing a change for the better. There is steady growth in the value of tourist arrivals, which today stands at about three million foreign tourists. The composition of tourists is also changing, with inflows from Europe, from where the vast majority of tourists come, stagnating, and tourists from Asian countries showing an increasing trend.

Indians are also increasingly travelling abroad in the post-liberalization era, both for work and pleasure. The entry of global brands in India, and international exposure through television has triggered off a desire to travel overseas. The vast increase in 'internet' usage is another factor that has accelerated exposure to the international environment.

Tourism has a lot of potential for expansion both in India and ASEAN countries, and also as an input in Indo-ASEAN services trade. Services, like trade, transport, communication and finance are the traditional components of the tertiary or service sector. Some of the newly emerging services are:

- Financial services.
- Marketing and communication services (media, advertising and consultancy).
- Marketing, logistics, trading and distribution.
- Trade promotion services.
- Government administration.
- Preventive health care services.
- Tourism.

Travel and tourism have emerged as the biggest industry of the millennium, according to John Nesbit in "Global Paradox". Besides direct employment, tourism is a multi-dimensional activity covering a large number of activities, such as travel agencies, souvenir shops, village handicrafts, preservation of historical monuments, and hotels. Tourism is thus a GDP accelerator. The "spread effects" of tourism is thus much wider. Tourism also helps survival of art forms, crafts and culture. Another feature is its contribution to national integration, and enrichment of the social and cultural lives of people. By 2020, there will be 1.6 billion international tourist arrivals worldwide, spending $2,000 million on tourism and auxiliary services. Between 2005 and 2010, 250 million new jobs would be created in this sector—200 million of them in the Asia-Pacific region alone.

The tourism revolution which has been sweeping the world since the 1960s has virtually by-passed India. Even after half a century of effort, India's share in the world tourism market has remained at a pathetic 0.64 percent, while ASEAN countries like Malaysia and Singapore have jumped to visitor counts, five to six times our figure.

The common strands in ASEAN countries tourism

performance are:

- Political will.
- Adequate infrastructure like hotels.
- Effective marketing and promotion.
- Tourism as a stand-alone activity, rather than an appendage.

China also is forging ahead in tourism promotion and considers tourism as a "pillar of the economy". Tourism in India is placed 51st in the Planning Commission's 52 priorities. However, after some recent pro-active steps by the Government of India, tourism has become the third largest foreign-exchange earner after gems and jewellery and ready-made garments, in the form of invisible exports. Tourism's contribution to foreign exchange during 2013 was ₹ 1,07,671 crore.

It is a well-known fact that tourism and the associated and ancillary services, which it generates, is a bigger money-spinner than the arms and armaments industry. However, only in recent years has the study of tourism and the hospitality industry received wider international attention. Today, hospitality and tourism is a global mega-industry and has been institutionalized as a socio-economic-ecological-cultural phenomenon. Income from tourism has tended to increase at a higher rate than merchandise exports in a number of countries. It acts as an assured channel of finance flow from developed to developing countries with serious balance of payments problems, because of its contributions to the "invisible" item in the balance of payments (BOP).

The more liberal vacation policies in big business organizations, greater affluence, and increase in spending among all sections of the people have given rise to an increased emphasis on leisure. The growing need for a change from routine social, business and family pressures has given tourism a greater importance. To leverage for the millennium, both the government and private sector need to do the following:

- Improve the quality of service. Tourism being a service

industry, the quality of service makes all the difference between competing destinations. A comprehensive HRD programme should cover: (a) orientation of staff at airports, (b) customs facilitation, and (c) guides on a continuous basis. Hygienic and efficient services will require a high degree of skill management, giving rise to more employment for improving training in diverse segments of the industry. Re-designing the tourism package should include in a greater measure the following.

- Adventure tourism—river-rafting, hang gliding.
- Wildlife tourism.
- Culture-specific tourism like heritage or Buddhist-circuit tourism—this will be of particular interest to Japan and ASEAN countries like Thailand.
- Create the right "image" abroad, by stressing India's uniqueness as a tourist destination, covering every taste and preference.
- There should be wide publicity and dissemination programmes to create awareness about India's diverse tourist attractions by innovative advertisements and promotional brochures.
- Himalayan mountains from Leh to Arunachal Pradesh would interest many young tourists from the ASEAN and the West, and should be marketed effectively.
- Due attention should be given to the highly individualistic and dietary selectivity of discerning foreigners, by highlighting India's rich variety of cuisine.
- India's cultural attaches in our embassies abroad should do much more to market India as a "unique" tourist destination, and should be effective as "cultural ambassadors".
- Easier accessibility by organizing: (i) more chartered flights, (ii) open skies policy—largely implemented with enhanced flights to ASEAN countries, and (iii) cleanliness, timely immigration processing and transparent customer service.

- Branding will play an increasingly important role when it comes to competition—The East India Hotels, (Oberoi Group) and Indian Hotels (Tatas) should develop proper synergies.
- Attention needs to be given to the small business travellers and IT professionals and their kith and kin, who are increasingly travelling abroad.
- Training facilities for tourist operators, travel agents and others connected with the industry needs to be strengthened to instil greater professionalism.

India has a vast cultural, cuisine and heritage diversity, but has not explored this to the extent it should in international markets. Singapore and India can exploit their synergies in marketing skills and capital investment for Singapore and promoting India's civilisational diversity.

The cultural attaches' of Indian High Commissions in Malaysia and Singapore and the Government of India tourism offices in Singapore and Kuala Lumpur have been co-operating with the local tourism promotion boards to promote India-ASEAN tourism. India is being projected not only as a cultural-heritage and holiday destination, but also for health (Ayurveda in Kerala and existence of state of the art reasonably-priced modern health care facilities in Indian cities, particularly Hyderabad) and adventure tourism.

Muslim pilgrims from Malaysia, Singapore and Indonesia are encouraged to halt in India on their way to Saudi Arabia for the Hajj pilgrimage. Indian and ASEAN tourism officials are also encouraging Buddhist tourists particularly from Thailand to visit Indian Buddhist centres in India, particularly in the Indian States of Bihar, Madhya Pradesh and Andhra Pradesh. Malaysia and Singapore are also now co-operating with each other to jointly promote their countries to tourists in India, rather than competing with each other.

Several crucial decisions in the Bali and Vientiane Indo-ASEAN Summits have been taken to permit direct flights by their respective carriers. The open-skies policy of India's civil aviation ministry is now being operationalised, with private carriers also being allowed to fly to ASEAN countries. Thus, greater connectivity between India and ASEAN will go a long way in enhancing the two-way tourist inflows, and commercial interaction.

Vietnam, Laos and Cambodia, can also attract an increasing number of tourists, with their heritage sites like Angkor Vat and Siem-Reap. Brunei and the Philippines can also attract Indian tourists, and India too needs to promote itself in a big way as these two countries are virtually untapped by tourist inflows from both sides.

A business-like pro-active approach is imperative in promoting tourism. An efficient and sound marketing strategy implying a systematic and co-coordinated execution of tourism policy by tourist undertakings, both government and private, is needed. A hard sell approach is the need of the hour to jointly market India's and ASEAN's tourism potential and get over the Westerner's view that Asia and India is a land of "snake charmers" and "rope tricks".

Lastly, Indians with higher incomes who travel abroad and interact with foreigners (including in ASEAN countries) tend to run-down India and project a negative image—this does more damage than all other promotional efforts to encourage tourism—this tendency needs to be put to an end, and all those of us who hear such people talking ill of India should severely be reprimanded. In conclusion, India and the ASEAN countries have great opportunities to exploit each other's synergies in the tourism sector.

References

Ahmed, E., "Regional Cooperation in South Asia and India's Role", *ISDA Journal*, New Delhi, 15(3), 1983.

Akrasanee, N., "ASEAN Economic Cooperation", in L.C. Martin, (ed.), The ASEAN Success Story: Social, Economic and Political Dimensions, Honolulu: East West Centre, 1987.

Ariff, M. and N. Hal., "Export Oriented Industrialisation in Sydney", Allen and Unwin, The ASEAN Experience, 1987.

ASEAN Round Table, "ASEAN Cooperation Agenda for the 1990s", Singapore: Institute for South East Asian Studies, 1987.

Baral, L., "SAARC but no 'SHARK' in South Asian Cooperation in Perspective", *Pacific Affairs,* 58(3), 1985.

Chng Meng Kng, "ASEAN's Institutional Structure and Economic Cooperation", *ASEAN Economic Bulletin*, 6(3), 1990.

Mehta, J.A., "The Regional Priorities", *Seminar*, New Delhi, 1983.

Mishra, P.K., "Towards a Framework of South Asian Regional Cooperation", *Foreign Affairs Reports,* New Delhi, 1982.

Wadhva, C.D., "Economic Cooperation among Countries of ASEAN and SAARC", Centre for Policy Research, 1988.

Wong, J., "ASEAN Experiences in Regional Economic Cooperation", *Asian Development Review,* 3(1), 1985.

4

India and South Asian Association for Regional Cooperation (SAARC)

The idea of setting up an organization for regional cooperation exclusively for seven South Asian nations—India, Bangladesh, Pakistan, Sri Lanka, Nepal, Bhutan and Maldives took shape in the early eighties. After the preparatory work of foreign secretaries was completed, it was decided that decisions should be taken on the basis of unanimity of all seven participating countries. It was agreed that contentious bilateral issues would be kept out of the deliberations, and regional cooperation would compliment multilateral cooperation. Following the preparatory meetings at the official and ministerial level, a summit meeting of the heads of states/governments was held in Dhaka in December 1985.The "Dhaka Declaration" was signed by the participating seven countries formally establishing SAARC (South Asian Association for Regional Cooperation).

SAARC Charter

The main objectives laid down by the SAARC chartor are the following:

1. To improve the quality of life and promote the welfare of the people of South Asia.
2. To accelerate economic growth and social and cultural development in the region.
3. To promote self-reliance among the countries of the South Asian region.
4. To generate mutual trust and understanding of each other's problems.
5. To promote cooperation and collaboration in economic, social, cultural, technical and scientific fields.
6. To strengthen cooperation with other LDCs.

7. To strengthen cooperation with regional and global organizations.

The second summit of SAARC was held in Bangalore in 1986. The "Bangalore Declaration" expressed concern at the deteriorating economic environment for South Asian countries, but there was no unanimity of view regarding expansion of the scope of SAARC for cooperation in the "core sector" activities such as trade, energy, money and finance. The Kathmandu summit of 1987 also had limited success in making specific commitment to enhancing intra-regional trade. So far, 17 SAARC summits have been held; the last one being held in Addu City, Maldives in 2011. The 18th summit would be held in Kathmandu in November 2014.

The 7th SAARC summit at Dhaka (1993) was postponed twice at the instance of India. The postponement of the summit was due to the volatile situation arising out of the demolition of the Babri Masjid in India.

The 15 page declaration adopted at the end of the summit in 1993 covered the following issues:

1. **South Asian Preferential Trade Area (SAPTA):** It was set up for economic cooperation in South Asia by liberalizing intra-region trade. The declaration called for gradual liberalization of intra-region trade and stressed the need for necessary steps to be taken to begin the first round of negotiations to exchange trade preferences among member states under SAPTA. The phrasing of the declaration related to liberalization of trade among SAARC members, and the signing of the framework of SAPTA are considered by analysts as a major concession to Pakistan.
2. **Terrorism:** The declaration stressed the need for coordinated action to combat terrorism. The SAARC leaders said that high priority should be given to the enactment of enabling legislation at the national level to help enforce the SAARC regional convention on suppression of terrorism. The member states, which had not yet done, so were urged to do so before the eighth

summit. All the member states excepting Pakistan and Bangladesh had enacted the enabling legislation.

The declaration also endorsed the integrated programme of action (IPA) on the eradication of poverty in South Asia, trade, manufacture and services, environment, population, shelter, children, youth, disabled persons, women's development, science and technology, drug trafficking, security of smaller states, people to people contact, and South Asian Development Fund (SADF).

New Delhi Summit

The eighth summit meeting of SAARC countries took place in New Delhi in 1995.The most important achievement of the summit was the agreement to operationalise SAPTA by December, 1995. However, the Indo-Pakistan hostility syndrome continued at the summit. The difficulties caused by asymmetry and related matters were on expected lines, but some other problems acquired new proportions. These, mainly related to the two "general provisions" of the SAARC charter: (i) decisions at all levels are to taken on the basis of unanimity and, (ii) bilateral and contentious issues are to be excluded from the deliberations. These decisions were taken after due deliberations and were based on sound logic. India attached great importance to consensus principle, if only to ensure that there was no ganging up of the others against it. This was also a safeguard for others, for was it inconceivable that any of the five or six countries would try to seek to push to the corner the remaining one or two? Similarly, the bar on contentious issues was intended to ensure that SAARC did not get bogged down in interminable controversies and shift the focus away from the basic objectives of regional cooperation.

Of late, Pakistan had sought to generate pressure against the bar. This was a part of its effort to internationalize its problems with India, especially the Kashmir issue—as against the bilateral approach favoured by India in terms of the commitment of the two sides under the Shimla agreement. It sought to win sympathy and support of the other members, saying that unresolved issues involving it and India had derailed the SAARC process and that the Association needed to address itself to the solution of these matters, if it was to forge ahead on the path of cooperation. This time, Nepal backed it on the issue. India, on the other hand, was opposed to any change in the charter. Though the SAARC forum was not to be used for bilateral matters, the opportunities provided by the presence of the heads of the summits, could be used—and had been used—for informal but valuable discussions.

There is so much divergence in the political perception of the SAARC countries, accentuated by extra-territorial powers who are interested in extending their influence in South Asia, that the very fact that member countries of SAARC have recognized that they can work together towards mutual advantage is in itself a big achievement. SAARC is much rhetoric about economic cooperation, but very little in terms of concrete programmes of enhancing trade or regional interaction.

South Asian Preferential Trade Area (SAPTA)

In order to increase intra-regional trade, a framework agreement on SAPTA was finalised by the Committee on Economic Cooperation, based on a draft prepared by the Inter-Governmental Group (IGG) on trade liberalization. This agreement was signed by the foreign ministers of all SAARC member states on 11th April, 1993. During the seventh SAARC summit in Dhaka, this agreement was an important landmark in the history of SAARC as it would go a long way in promoting intra-regional trade and in gradually removing trade barriers existing in the member countries.

The basic principles of SAPTA are as follows:

1. Overall reciprocity and mutuality of advantages.
2. Step-by-step negotiations and extensions of preferential trade arrangement in stages.
3. Inclusion of all types of products—raw, semi-processed and processed.
4. Special and favourable treatment to least developed

countries (LLDCs). The special treatment to LLDCs include allowance of favourable percentage points, application of relaxed rules of origin, favourable terms of technical assistance, duty free access, deeper tariff preferences, removal of non-tariff and para-tariff barriers, negotiations of long-term contracts to support sustainable exports and provision of special facilities with regard to shipping and identification, preparation and establishment of industrial and agricultural projects, training facilities and support to export marketing etc., possibly linked to cooperative financing and buyback arrangements.

SAPTA is expected to benefit not only the LDC members, but also the economically stronger members because of pooling of resources and markets, lower transport and transit costs due to geographical contiguity, relative compatibility of capital and intermediate goods produced within the region to factor endowments of other member states, efficiency gains due to increased intra-regional competition, and amicable environment for political harmony created as economic ties grow stronger and consequent benefits gain significance.

Expanded intra-regional trade and joint ventures can offer larger potential benefits to South Asia, which comprises about one-fifth of the world population. Natural resources endowments along with availability of relatively less expensive manpower in the region at all skill levels ensure benefits in terms of larger markets and fuller utilization of production capabilities, transfer of technology and comparative advantages.

The opening up of transit facilities under SAPTA would also necessitate harmonization of trading and commercial documents as well as the exact definition of the rules of origin of the trade goods. Both these developments would stimulate intra-regional trade still further.

Pakistan, India and SAARC

As a consequence of the Islamabad SAARC Summit of 2004, and the Indo-Pakistan dialogue, Pakistan seems to be at last, looking for a realistic solution to the Kashmir dispute. There was thus a "paradigm shift" in that country's "bleed India" policy. However, experience of the past shows that any forward movement in peace initiatives is followed by retracting to old positions of animosity and hostility. Pakistan often talks peace, while preparing for war. It is hoped that the "war of attrition" in Kashmir will be given a final burial. The raison-de-atre of the Pakistan State should change from being a "spoiler" of India's progress. Pakistan should not insist on Kashmir as the core issue and progress with talks with India sequentially, but veer around to the Indian viewpoint that talks should progress simultaneously on all issues, including economic co-operation. Economic co-operation can bind the two nations together, unlike politics, which will create further divisions and mutual distrust.

Whatever be the motives, Pakistan is moving at a pace no one had dreamt of before. The voices within Pakistan urging the establishment to look for a way out of the Kashmir imbroglio are feeble, but growing. This could mean that the high-pitched decades-old rhetoric is toned down. Negotiations, from a Pakistan point of view should be conducted with India on a LoC (Line of Control) plus solution that allows for some territorial adjustments and soft borders, and possibly a ten-mile deep de-militarized zone. While the division of Kashmir was unfortunate, it is better to accept this reality, than live with endless suffering that has consumed almost a million lives since the 1980s.

However, there is a growing feeling in Pakistan that the country was being made to give in too much, without anything in return from India. It is hoped that once the "composite dialogue" gets underway, the feeling that India is extracting concessions from Pakistan without commensurate benefits is put to rest. In its assessment, the Indian government feels there is unlikely to be any change in Pakistan's position vis-à-vis India. Kashmir is not about to be toppled off its pedestal, and a significant component of the Pakistan military intelligence establishment will continue to subscribe to the "bleed India theory". Given the poor state of the Pakistan economy, anyone who comes to power in Pakistan is likely to be more vulnerable to the same pressures from the U.S. and other Western powers.

The 12th Summit of SAARC took place in the context of complex social, economic and political developments globally and regionally. The slowing down of global trade negotiations under WTO, a "shining India", and in some measure South Asia, the success of formations like ASEAN, the increasing international pressure to combat terrorism and resolve regional conflicts and regional security concerns have contributed to making regionalism not an option, but a necessity especially among LDCs with a burgeoning growth potential. But in the past, SAARC nations have been lackadaisical about implementing the high-sounding commitments of Summit declarations. The question to be asked is—"is there any reason to believe that the Islamabad summit has discovered the magic that will hasten the pace towards regional integration"?

As has often been pointed out, SAARC is after all a unique regional group in many ways and especially because one country, India, constitutes a centrality that is physical, geographical and economic. And there lies the core of the problem. The strongest gains of regionalism naturally accrue to India. It is for India to ensure that smaller members of the region have a growing stake in regionalism as well. This responsibility India has taken seriously. For example, SAFTA (South Asia Free Trade Agreement) envisages the liberalisation of commodity trade as a key issue, with trade in services following.

As critics have pointed out, this would have little appeal to smaller nations, which only feel threatened by the flooding of goods from India, with the removal of barriers. Little effort has been made to ensure necessary protection to the least developed countries of the region. It is here that enlarging co-operation in areas such as education and health services can create synergies. It is also a cause for concern that SAARC agreements on co-operation on other issues, which attract no barriers, have not taken off. In 1992, the "Poverty Commission Report of SAARC" set the target for the eradication of poverty in South Asia. All that happened was that in 2002, another commission was constituted, that came up with further recommendations. Nor have SAARC nations registered a commendable record in other areas of possible co-operation. Under the "Integrated Programme of Action", there has not been a single co-operative project to harness hydro potential in the region for mutual benefit despite talk of sub-regional co-operation through growth triangles or quadrangles between India's Northeast, Bangladesh, Bhutan and Nepal.

Assessment of SAARC

SAARC would complete thirty years of its existence in 2015. The countries of South Asia have great diversity in the levels of industrialization. Thus, trade in industrial goods through advantages of increased competitiveness may not take place. However, these are similarities in the major exportable items where regional cooperation is beneficial. In Bangladesh and India, jute and tea are important export commodities; in Pakistan and India cotton; and between Sri Lanka and India, tea; and between all countries of the region, textiles, garments and leather goods are important exportables. Trade in complementary items can lead to country/commodity specialization, sharing of sales and marketing information, and jointly exploring third-country markets.

The intensity of trade among South Asian countries is low and between ASEAN and SAARC sub-regions only marginally better, with a strong bias in all these countries to trade with industrialized extra-regional countries. The intra-regional trade among SAARC countries is low because besides having a "colonial propensity" there is added disadvantage of the perceived "India hegemony" factor. The countries of South Asia fear that India, being the dominant economic power of the region, she would be the only beneficiary in trade liberalization and economic cooperation projects.

The political scenario in South Asia is complex, with both regional and extra-regional strategic interests adding to friction and hence limiting greater regional economic integration. The "Shared Security Perception", which is a sine quo non of successful integration in other areas of the world is totally non-existent in the SAARC sub-region. India has had major political differences with almost all her South Asian neighbours, with the exception of Bhutan and Maldives. Some of the problems are due to the colonial legacy of a "common nation", while others relate to ethnic issues, sharing of river waters, differences over extra-regional powers and their relative roles, and the very fact that India is geographically and economically the pre-eminent regional power.

Thus, SAARC meetings have been much talk and common intent of good will, but have not gone beyond peripheral issues like a common approach to drug trafficking, the environment, or a desire for a world free of nuclear weapons. SAARC nations have to work on the principle of the "lowest common denominator" and proceed cautiously through consultation, before they embark on substantial economic cooperation.

Analysts feel that cooperation among SAARC nations faces the following obstacles:

1. The ongoing political situation in the region is not conducive to cooperation. The traditional rivalry between India and Pakistan and the political climate in other countries points towards the unstable condition in the region.
2. The security problem in the region remains unresolved. India insists that regional security should be tackled through bilateral talks within the region and without the involvement of external powers. India's views is shared by Bhutan and Maldives, but Pakistan, Bangladesh and Sri Lanka, view India as a security threat and favour the presence of external powers in the region.

3. The imbalance in the resource position among SAARC members is seen as an obstacle to meaningful cooperation. Mutual suspicion of dependency has caused the member states to follow divergent development strategies.
4. The inter-mingling of the people of the region remains elusive, and on the contrary, each country tries to maintain its separate identity.
5. Political instability within the SAARC countries is another reason for poor cooperation among its members.
6. Despite the drawbacks to cooperation, SAARC cannot be written off. The SAARC summits have started the process of regional discussion and cooperation which over a period of time can create lasting bonds of friendship and cooperation among member States. The future of SAARC, however, will be determined more by bilateral relations among its member States.

On the flip side, the disadvantages would be that India would have to constantly bend backwards to accommodate other smaller neighbours. Also, India's natural strategic compass is broader than South Asia, and extends from the Straits of Hormuz to the Malaccan Straits, with a pre-eminent role as a global power. Open borders also may spell trouble—we will have a flood of illegal immigrants particularly from Bangladesh and Pakistan, which may retard the Indian economy.

Coming to the specifics of SAFTA, it is on the whole a welcome step, as tariff barriers in the region are all artificial. However, the duration of the process is too long. The process started in 2006 and continues for another 6 to 8 years before the tariffs are actually brought down to the minimum range. The pace is much slower than the WTO route, and not keeping in pace with worldwide liberalisation trends. Sri Lanka has a FTA (Free Trade Agreement) with India and Pakistan, and will be initialling one with Bangladesh.

In the current global context of regionalism, SAFTA will attract wider global attention in view of the combined huge market size and the growth potential of the region in terms of available resources. South Asia has multiple heterogeneities, namely geographical, economic, political and social. The region doesn't lack resources, but lacks initiatives for building complementarities.

SAARC region continues to remain a hub of poverty, large unemployment, and economic backwardness. On the macro economic front, all the major economies suffer from large fiscal deficits; expenditure increases on account of defence and security.

SAARC was established in 1986 as recognition of the imperative for a wider and broad-based regional co-operation forum encompassing cultural, social, economic and technical fields. However, SAARC couldn't make much headway ever since its inception, as each country followed a development strategy independent of others, without any policy co-ordination. Intra-SAARC trade has made little headway.

Even if India is a dominant economy in SAARC, it makes tremendous economic sense to enter into co-operation with India. Since India is an emerging fast moving economy, the smaller countries can stand to benefit immensely by accessing the large domestic market of India. It should give them great opportunities for developing their economies, particularly agriculture and industry.

However, we should also integrate investment with trade. Bangladesh will sell to India in a free trade environment Dacca saris or hilsa fish, in which it has a competitive advantage and ready demand in India. But this will be a lop-sided trade practice, defeating the very process. If India invests in gas-based projects in Bangladesh, and later imports gas from that country, it will be much more meaningful in a South Asian context.

Apart from trade, there will be the larger "peace and stability dividend". There will be region wide growth, peace and harmony and a more conducive environment for investment, employment, effective resource mobilisation and utilisation for all countries.

A breakthrough in Indo-Pak bilateral relations is more good news for the "economic health" of the region, and will vindicate intra-SAARC trade liberalisation. Pharmaceuticals, engineering goods, power and infrastructure are areas of immediate intra-regional co-operation.

Will SAFTA work in the long-run? Today, NAFTA is working well, EU's (European Union) single market and single currency have been very successful and of course ASEAN is working very well. There is thus reason to hope that SAARC will also be successful.

The progress in SAPTA was stymied and marred by apprehension, especially in Bangladesh and Pakistan, regarding possible flooding of goods from India. The focus of the trade dialogue within the region is dominated more by the desire to balance bilateral trade, than by the desire to promote trade. This comes in the way of growth of trade and affects progress on SAPTA/SAFTA.

Intra-SAARC investments are not very significant. Instead of co-operating among themselves, they have been competing to attract FDI. There is lack of dynamism at present in the intra-SAARC trade relationship.

The intermeshing of Indian and Singaporean areas of concern in trade augurs well for both countries. Singapore is looking out for viable and lucrative destinations besides China and the US, and India is well placed both economically and diplomatically to forge an effective and mutually beneficial partnership. Thus, the increasing diplomatic complementarities and synergies of the two countries in trade and investment, will act as a stabilizing force in the Asia-Pacific region.

The idea of setting up an organisation for regional cooperation exclusively for the seven South Asian countries—India, Bangladesh, Pakistan, Sri Lanka, Nepal, Bhutan and Maldives—took shape in the early 1980s. After the preparatory work of foreign secretaries was completed, it was decided that decisions should be taken on the basis of unanimity of all seven participating countries. It was agreed that contentious bilateral issues would be kept out of the deliberations, and regional cooperation would complement multilateral cooperation. Following the preparatory meeting at the official and ministerial level, a summit meeting of the Heads of State/Government was held in Dhaka in December 1985. The "Dhaka Declaration" was signed by the participating seven countries, thus formally establishing SAARC (South Asian Association for Regional Cooperation).

A charter for SAARC was formulated, where objectives and methods of cooperation were worked out. Among the objectives, emphasis is given to acceleration of economic growth, and promotion and strengthening of collective self-reliance among the South Asian nations. Among the objectives is also the promotion of active collaboration and mutual assistance in economic, social, cultural, technical and scientific fields. Given the amount of divergence in the political perception of the SAARC countries, accentuated by extra-territorial powers who are interested in extending their influence in South Asia, the very fact that member countries of SAARC have recognised that they can work together towards mutual advantage is in itself a big achievement. SAARC is thus much rhetoric about economic cooperation, but very little in terms of concrete programmes of enhancing trade or regional interaction.

ASEAN and SAARC: An Assessment

The countries of South Asia have great diversity in the levels of industrialisation. Thus, trade in industrial goods through advantages of increased competitiveness may not take place. There are, however, similarities in the major exportable items, where regional cooperation is beneficial. In Bangladesh and India, jute and tea are important export commodities; in Pakistan and India, cotton; between Sri Lanka and India, tea; and between all countries of the region, textiles, garments, and leather goods are important exportables. Trade in complementary items can lead to country/commodity specialisation, sharing of sales and marketing information, and jointly exploring third-country markets.

The intensity of trade among South Asian countries is low and between ASEAN and SAARC sub-regions only marginally better, with a strong bias in all these countries to trade in all these countries to trade with industrialised extra-regional countries.

The intra-regional trade among SAARC countries is low because besides having a "colonial propensity" there is the added disadvantage of the perceived "India hegemony" factor. The countries of South Asia fear that India, being the dominant economic power of the region, which would be the only beneficiary in trade liberalisation and economic projects.

The political scenario in South Asia is complex, with both regional and extra-regional strategic interests adding to friction and hence limiting greater regional integration. The "shared security perception", which is a sine qua non of successful integration in other areas of the world, is non-existent in the SAARC sub-region. India has had major political differences with almost all her South Asian neighbours, with the exception of Bhutan and Maldives. Some of the problems are due to the colonial legacy of a common "nation", while others relate to ethnic issues, sharing of river waters, differences over extra-regional powers and their relative roles, and the very fact that India is geographically and economically the pre-eminent regional power. SAARC meetings have been much talk and common intent of good will, but have not gone beyond peripheral issues like a common approach to drug trafficking, environment or a desire for a world free of nuclear weapons. SAARC nations have to work on the principle of "lowest common denominator" and proceed cautiously through consultation, before they embark on substantial areas of economic cooperation.

ASEAN too, though much more successful than SAARC in overcoming regional misperceptions and animosities, has encountered problems in each major area of economic cooperation. The preferential trading arrangements (PTAs) have items with little trading significance. The large-scale ASEAN industrial projects have achieved only limited progress. The soda ash project in Thailand and the copper fabrication project in the Philippines have failed to "take off". The industrial complementation programmes, envisaged to promote intra-regional division of labour, have been non-starters. Although the three main parts of the industrialisation strategy of ASEAN did not lead to substantial capital formation, the investment climate within ASEAN did succeed in attracting substantial foreign direct investment (FDI). The PMCs (Post-Ministerial Conferences), in which discussions take place with dialogue partners following their annual meetings, have been quite successful. ASEAN has achieved remarkable diplomatic cohesion, but should promote regional efforts to bolster cooperation and consultation and improve regional programmes to take advantage of regional markets and complementarities.

SAARC and ASEAN can develop interactive relationships, and have greater avenues for cooperation through exploiting inter-regional complementarities, joint ventures, and joint production and commodity marketing strategies.

To sum up, regional cooperation can take on more meaningful dimensions only if political barriers to closer economic relations are overcome. ASEAN has been more successful than SAARC primarily because of the "shared security perception" or the political CET (Common External Threat) factor. The economic CET (Common External Tariff) factor has always followed the political CET factor in all successful regional organisations. The perceived "economic domination" by India, which is the main stumbling block for greater intra-SAARC trade, should be overcome by step-by-step selective tariff liberalisation on products of interest to all countries of the sub-region. Once intra-SAARC trade gathers momentum, SAARC and ASEAN can work together, as role models for successful South-South cooperation and peace in the Indian Ocean region.

Regional cooperation in the Indian Ocean region for peace encompasses the other two major regional organisations as well—GCC in West Asia and SADCC in Southern Africa as well. A network of cooperative and synergetic regional organisations is the first step to forming an "Indian Ocean Community". We also firmly believe that regional cooperation schemes involve more directly people of the region and thus joint ventures in small-scale enterprises with locally and regionally available human and national resources should get top priority.

5

India and Asia-Pacific Economic Cooperation (APEC) Forum

APEC forum is poised to become the dominant economic force in the dynamic Asia-Pacific region, where there is growing interdependence, based on growing trade and investment ties. APEC has considerable diversity, and is far from being a homogenous group. The eighteen countries in the region have differences, which range from culture to legal and political structures, and to stages of economic development. This diversity of the countries in the region has been an important factor in curbing the creation of an institutional arrangement encompassing the entire region, where similar regional arrangements have progressed in other parts of the world. The countries range from the small, but natural resource rich nations of Brunei and Papua New Guinea, to the large and economically powerful U.S. and Japan.

There are the dynamic newly industrializing countries (NICs) of South Korea, Taiwan, Singapore and Hong Kong, which have had the world's highest growth rates in this group. The rapidly growing second generation NICs of ASEAN (Association of Southeast Asian Nations)—Malaysia, Thailand and Indonesia are also members of APEC. China, despite its present low per capita income, stands apart because of its size, expanding market and high growth potential. The South American members, Mexico and Chile have little in common with others, besides sharing a Pacific coastline and experiencing fairly rapid growth rates, although they have recently had difficulties in macro economic management. Canada, Australia and New Zealand are the other three industrially advanced "white members" of the group. Within APEC, the distance between the richest and poorest countries is very large with Japan's per capita income almost sixty times larger than China, and the U.S. and Papua New Guinea at almost opposite ends of the world's GNP table.

Divisive Issues in APEC

Many trade and other disputes divide the member countries. The U.S. and Japan narrowly skirted a full-scale trade war because of serious differences over protecting the U.S. market from Japanese automobile exports. Japan slapped an anti-dumping clause on China.

Japan, Korea and Taiwan do not want to open up their agricultural trade, because of strong domestic farm lobbies, much to the annoyance of U.S. and Australia. Malaysia wants to push ahead with its EAEC (East Asian Economic Caucus), an economic grouping sans the U.S. There are also serious differences between China and Taiwan and South Korea and Japan.

The Japanese whose brand of "Mercantilism" is much criticised by the U.S. feels that it can rally behind it the countries of Northeast and Southeast Asia, if there is a trade confrontation with the U.S., and is in the process of developing an "Asian Consciousness", and projecting its version of consultative consensus in international trade dealings.

However, there is also a conflicting trend of an underlying distrust for Japan because of its pre-World War II exploitative imperial record in Asia, and the fear of revival of the "Greater East Asian Co-Prosperity Sphere", with all its negative connotations. Chinese expansionism is also suspect.

Its effective combination of defiance and deal making in its interactions with the U.S., despite serious differences, and its expanding military prowess evokes feelings of fear and mistrust among its smaller neighbours in Asia.

Open Regionalism

APEC was set up primarily as a consultative framework and an ongoing process, not as a regional institutional grouping, or as a retaliatory exclusive trade bloc. The forum is based on "open regionalism" containing elements of both regional and global approaches to issues.

Regionalism is today fast catching on in the world. According to WTO, 110 regional deals were notified to GATT between 1948 and 1995. 1995 saw the accession to the European Union (EU), the world's biggest trading bloc of Austria, Finland and Sweden, and the creation of Mercosur, a customs union between Argentina, Brazil, Paraguay and Uruguay. SAPTA (South Asian Preferential Trade Area) has come into being in South Asia.

The seven ASEAN nations agreed to set up a free trade area by 2003. Slovenia would join the Czech Republic, Hungary, Poland and Slovakia in the Central European Free-Trade Area. The EU and Turkey would also set up a customs union.

Thus, regional deals can accelerate liberalisation of things partially covered by WTO—for example the protection of foreign direct investment (FDI).

Regional forums are also more flexible, as problems that would take years to sort out in global talks, can be dealt with in much shorter periods, where lesser number of countries are involved. Regional trade deals also "lock in" liberalisation, especially in LDCs (Less Developed Countries).

APEC, despite fissiparous tendencies has come to stay as a viable grouping because of "open regionalism".

This means promoting the integration of the Asia-Pacific region, while avoiding needless discrimination against the rest of the world.

APEC by being an "open non-discriminatory economic association" has as its primary focus, economic or more specially trade issues. It is also a "voluntary association" in which coordinated decision-making is based on consensus, rather than an attempt to impose any supra-regional authority on its participants.

Traditional trade barriers such as tariffs or quotas need not be the only strategic obstacles to mutually beneficial integration of the Asia-Pacific region. The reduction of these barriers needs to be accompanied by work to reduce transaction costs imposed by uncertainties and infrastructure problems, as well as incompatible standards, regulations and administrative procedures. APEC governments should continue to follow the MFN (Most Favoured Nation) principle of Article 1 of GATT/WTO rather than trying to accommodate APEC through Article 24 of GATT, which would lead to diversion of effort to convert APEC into a formal organisation delaying actual liberalisation.

Osaka Declaration

The "Osaka Declaration" or more specially the "Action Agenda" has as its defining feature "voluntarism" and "political determination" or as Malaysia prefers to call it controversially yet accurately "non-binding commitments". The "Osaka Initial Actions" and teeth to the Bogor Declaration were meant to resolving the developed APEC members to remove barriers to trade by 2010 and the developing members by 2020. The term "initial actions" reflects a political will among APEC members, who are required to officially reveal them only while declaring their action plans at their annual meeting in the Philippines next year. The fact that they have chosen to do so, albeit in tentative form, a full year earlier lends weight to the comment of the former Australian Prime Minister, Paul Keating, who said "it is the only body in the world that holds up prospects of general trade liberalisation".

The APEC has working groups on trade and investment, data review, trade promotion, industrial science and technology, HRD (human resource development), regional energy cooperation, marine resources conservation, telecommunications, transportation, tourism and fisheries. The APEC has agreed to permit non-members to participate in working groups as guests. Participation in the WG (working groups) must be clearly understood not to imply any tacit endorsement of future membership or observers' status in other APEC activities.

The subject that dominated APEC and the Action Agenda was that of trade and investment liberalisation in 15 areas, to the disappointment of the developing economies like Indonesia and the Philippines, who preferred greater thrust on economic and technical cooperation.

China agreed to slash substantially the tariff on over 4,000 items by 1996. The reduction of the simple average tariff will be no less than 30 percent.

Japan announced that it will raise the number of tariff reductions from 400 to 700, including textiles, chemicals, and steel and non-ferrous metals, to be completed two years earlier than the January 1998 date agreed in the Uruguay Round of GATT.

Aspects of the APEC agenda include improving communications, reducing uncertainties, resolving disputes, harmonising commercial laws and regulations, setting standards, meeting global objectives and taking the lead in global negotiations.

India's Standing in APEC

India has to sit up and brace herself to face the emerging realities, with the centre of the world's economy moving rightward i.e. to the Pacific, and APEC poised to become the dominant economic force in the dynamic Asia-Pacific region.

India's isolation from the wider efforts at Asian regional cooperation is a matter of great disappointment. India's excessive preoccupation with sub-continental problems, the fact that she was a late starter in the liberalisation process, and the lack of diplomatic and commercial dynamism in cultivating ASEAN in its formative years, has resulted in a more reactive rather than a pro-active stance with regard to APEC.

India sounded out countries like Singapore, South Korea and Australia of its interest in being a part of APEC, after the ban on its expansion. The Prime Minister of India in his Singapore lecture stated that "the Asia-Pacific should be the spring board for India's leap into the global market place. In the market-driven export-oriented economy of the future, India has a lot to gain by aligning closely with the APEC countries".

However, at the Osaka APEC summit, it was decided that at

the Manila summit to be held in 1996, non-member countries would be permitted to participate in working group discussions, but not at the summit level conference. This does not improve any country's chance of gaining membership, but gives it an opportunity to network with other members and influence decisions. Japan, Hong Kong and Singapore were apprehensive about the criteria to be approved for new membership after the end of 1996, when the Seattle meeting, specifying embargo on expansion would end. It is still unclear whether the new members should meet the defined criteria or depend on various other considerations—first the new members will be identified and then the criteria tailored to fit their inclusion.

India also needs to be taken move seriously because by 2005, India would be able to export goods worth US$ 90 billion, and the country's share of world trade will be 1.1 percent. India should also be a buyer of goods worth US$ 90 billion annually, a market that cannot be ignored. Even the World Bank has identified India as becoming the fourth largest economy in purchasing power parity (PPP), terms by 2020. India's attitude towards East Asia will also decade India's admission into APEC more than not, in very significant trade volumes.

More than 50 percent of India's trade passes through the Pacific. Thus, it is interested in APEC and has a stake in the security and stability of East Asia and the Pacific.

The Indian Parliament also should be taken into confidence about what obligations India's membership of APEC entails by way of tariff reductions. India should also take note of the fact that a surrender or loss of some of its sovereignty would be more than made up by taking away some of other's sovereignty.

Besides her economic potential, military strength and physical size, in sheer geographical terms, India abuts on both ASEAN and APEC. China has a long border with India, and Indonesia is barely 100 miles away from the southernmost island of the Andaman's chain. Three of ASEAN's seven members have maritime boundaries with India. There are many native Indians in Malaysia and Singapore, and in cultural terms too, India has close affinity with Indonesia and Malaysia. Non-resident Indian nationals are also playing a significant role in the U.S., Canadian and Australian economies.

Political Relations between India and the APEC Countries

India, seen through the Cold War prism of Southeast Asia was perceived as a country mired in sub-continental problems, steeped in poverty due to obsolete economic approaches and an unacceptable strategic relationship with the former Soviet Union. India has a historic opportunity to unshackle itself from these past misconceptions and demonstrate the necessary political will and capability to play a constructive role in the dynamic Asia-Pacific region.

ASEAN's support for India in the region though primarily based on India's attractiveness as an emerging market, is also important in geo-political terms as a factor in China's containment, and an assertion of its autonomy vis-à-vis the U.S. in the ARF (ASEAN Regional Forum).

The U.S. and India have in fact congruent geo-political interests in maintaining a fair and stable equilibrium in Asia. India also needs to further alter its perception that the U.S. has an interest in creating impediments in its overall progress. The U.S. has been asking India to share its strategic concerns in the Asia-Pacific, particularly regarding the challenge China poses as an emerging Asian super power, and also the possibility of instability and uncertainty in the Korean peninsular. The U.S. and India have been exploring the possibility of closer military co-operation since the 1991 Kickleighter proposals. The trouble with the U.S. is that it is not sensitive to India's strategic concerns in relation to Pakistan, particularly with regard to the Kashmir issue. The U.S. continues to view Pakistan as a frontline moderate Islamic state, and a strategic ally to counter insurgency and fundamentalism in West and Central Asia. It is not willing to accommodate India's concerns about Pakistan's nuclear and missile capabilities, and to accept India as a strategic ally, with the new equations in the post-Cold War world. Pakistan has adroitly managed to keep India out of the U.S.'s. primary foreign policy concerns.

China's growing military and economic prowess also poses a threat to India, as also its nuclear and missile capability in conjunction with Pakistan. The U.S. again is not sensitive to India's concerns regarding China. However, at the same time India does not want to identify too closely with the U.S. confrontationist stance towards China, which may prove to be counter-productive in the relaxed bilateral context of Sino-Indian relations. The 'Border Dispute' between the two countries has for all purposes between frozen, and there is growing economic interaction between the two countries. There is thus primarily a mismatch of perceptions and expectations between India on the one hand as an emerging regional power and the U.S. on the other hand as a global power, which may not be sufficiently attuned to India's sensitivities and concerns.

Added to this is China's emergence as a power with a global outreach—hence, the differing perceptions in the Asia-Pacific region. It is in India's long-term interest that she consolidates her "Asian identity". The ASEAN resilient approach of consultative and constructive engagement towards China to deter it from pursuing an aggressive and expansionist course suits India's interest the most. India must also keep in mind that support for its ARF application came from the ASEAN economies, despite the U.S., Canada, Japan and Australia wanting India to soften her stand on global non-proliferation issues like CTBT before agreeing to India playing a larger role in the Asia-Pacific region. However, apart from the nuclear issue, India's diplomatic ties are being further strengthened with Australia, Canada and Japan who all recognise it as an emerging economic force in Asia, which can compete with China.

Recent initiatives taken by India have gone a long way in removing apprehensions about India's intentions and capability of her military in the Asia-Pacific region. Joint naval exercises with Australia, Malaysia, Singapore and Indonesia have definitely contributed to a better understanding of the realities. Strategic co-operation received further fillip when India and Malaysia signed a Memorandum of Understanding in defence cooperation. Malaysian Air force personnel are being trained in the use of MIG 29 aircraft. The India-Malaysia dialogue and the Indo-Thailand dialogue have agreed that co-operation should include joint production and development of defence equipment.

India has however to realise that despite removal of apprehensions regarding military capabilities, India is the only country in the APEC region which is not a signatory to the NPT (Nuclear Non-Proliferation Treaty) or any other nuclear restraint regime. India's isolation by not signing the CTBT is viewed with great concern. There may be pressures on India to endorse the Southeast Asia Nuclear Weapons' Free Zone (SEANWFZ) and possibly become a part of it.

Even India's approach towards Pakistan will be expected to be compatible with overall confidence building, conflict-resolution, and preventive diplomacy culture of the Asia-Pacific region. India's relationship with Russia will be closely watched, as any new arms acquisitions and up-gradation. India has to articulate her security concerns with extreme caution. China and the U.S. can pursue their respective security and nuclear policies though they are incompatible with ASEAN's primary concerns, but India may not be treated with the same circumspection. India will evoke more respect in the region, if she acts confidently and pursues a more pro-active Asia-Pacific diplomatic policy, and goes ahead with her domestic liberalisation policies with full vigour, and strengthens economic links with APEC nations.

Conclusions

India should identify her core competitiveness in various commodities of interest to the APEC countries. Niche markets should be developed in exports such as textiles, gems and jewellery and leather goods. New forms of cooperation like trade -generating joint ventures and joint tendering for third country projects with some of APEC economies, should be pursued with renewed vigour.

With the United States, India should intensify and diversify her economic relationship. As one of India's largest trading partner and also the largest investor, U.S. economic policy have very important implications for the Indian economy. U.S. involvement in the development of the crucial infrastructure areas of the Indian economy like power, telecommunications, energy and transport should be deepened. In commodity trade, besides traditional commodities where India has a brand equity advantage, new products like engineering and software exports should be exported in larger quantities.

With the near normalisation of relations with China, cross-border trade should get a boost and the vast Chinese market should be very attractive for Indian exporters. Cooperation should also be intensified in areas like small industries and the financial sector, where India has considerable expertise.

In response to the continued rapid progress on market reforms, Australia's department of foreign affairs and trade has sharpened the commercial focus of the country's approach to India, while actively promoting the full range of the relationship. The Japanese also are showing renewed interest in India, and investment which was a bit slow in coming to India in the past should accelerate in the near future. There are also immense possibilities for a fruitful economic relationship with South Korea. The competitive advantage of South Korea in ship building, port management and automobile manufacturing has many lessons for India. The "Chaebols" (large industrial conglomerates) also can share their expertise with Indian companies in their globalising efforts.

In order to strengthen her case for APEC membership, India should press ahead in economic reforms with renewed vigour. Greater liberalisation and incentives for foreign investment should send the right signals to investors in these countries. Full convertibility of the rupee, rationalisation of taxes, and fulfilling her international obligations, in WTO (World Trade Organisation), should help in accelerating India's global integration with APEC.

India should also keep herself fully informed of the

deliberations and recommendations of APEC committees. There should be regular consultations with APEC member countries in international fora like the UN, IMF and WTO, where India should use all her diplomatic finesse to align her viewpoint with these countries.

India has much to gain from APEC in terms of trade reciprocity. As Indian trade barriers are demolished in relation to APEC, it will result in APEC also removing the trade barriers.

There are many commodities in which India and APEC may complement each other on the basis of their respective surpluses and deficits. One serious short-term bottleneck may be posed by the insufficient availability of exportable surplus from India in a member of items. This may be overcome by greater inflows of investments from APEC to India in line with the "flying geese" model of shifting comparative advantage.

At present, APEC does not take much cognizance of the existence of the South Asia region. Regional cooperation facilitates the process of national integration, as has been seen from ASEAN experience in its formative years. If South Asia can start moving ahead jointly, after burying mutual animosity and discord, there is no reason why it cannot turn into a more dynamic entity, which can evolve over time into a cooperative partner of APEC. Cooperation with APEC will also further reinforce the process of intra-SAARC integration.

On the part of APEC also, it is necessary to recognise the huge potential of India, for investment-related trade with its large market and vast repository of natural and human resources, which can be profitably exploited for mutual benefit.

Thus, India's desire to join APEC will depend on her diplomatic skills, and the economic and political clout she can muster before the next APEC summit.

APEC should also move further towards realising a region-wide open economy, which will not only contribute to regional liberalization of trade and investment, but will also advance the goal of global free trade. At the same time, APEC should be willing to meet the challenge of maintaining a sound and balanced economic relationship between the eastern and western parts of the Pacific. Individual APEC member countries' active participation in further unilateral liberalization, open-regionalism, region-wide trade facilitation programmes and cooperative efforts for structural transformation would greatly expedite the process of meeting this challenge successfully.

APEC should take steps in evolving into a positive force and role-model for global liberalisation through 'open regionalism', rather than yet another threat to the global system.

References

APEC, "Achieving the APEC Vision: Free and Open Trade in the Asia-Pacific", Second Report of the Eminent Persons Group, August, 1994.

APEC, "APEC Economic Leaders' Declaration of Common Resolve", Bogor, Indonesia, November, 1994.

Balls, Edward, "Divining the Motives for U.S.-Japan Bashing", Financial Times, London, 19th July, 1993.

Bhanoji Rao, V.V., "APEC Perspectives and India", *The Economic Times*, Bombay, 10th October, 1994.

Dobson, Wendy, "APEC Cooperation Amidst Diversity", ASEAN Economic Bulletin, Vol. 10, No. 3, 1994.

Elek, Andrew, "APEC Beyond Bogor: An Open Economic Association in the Asian-Pacific Region", Asian-Pacific Economic Literature, Vol. 9, No. 1, 1995.

Ganekar, Bhagyashree, "Indo-Korean Cooperation: A Blooming Symbiosis", *The Economic Times*, 26th February, 1996.

Garnaut, R, "Options for Asia-Pacific Trade Liberalisation: A Pacific Free Trade Area"?, in China, Siow Yue (ed.), APEC: Challenges and Opportunities, ISEAS, Singapore, 1994.

Jayanth, V., "Unrealised Potential of Indo-Australian Trade", *The Hindu*, March 28th, 1996.

Jiali, Ma, "Relations between China and India Towards 21st Century", ICAPS Conference, Hyderabad, 1996.

Khergamvala, F.J, "APEC Steps to Remove Trade Barriers", *The Hindu*, 18th November, 1995.

Malhotra, Inder, "India, APEC, ASEAN and ARF", *The Times of India*, 23rd November, 1994.

Naisbitt, John, "Mega Trends Asia", Nicholas Brealey Publishing, London, 1995.

Reza, Sadrel, "Economic Policy Reforms in South Asia and SAARC-APEC Trade Cooperation", DEVINSA South Asian Reviews and Abstracts, Vol. 7, No. 6, Marga Institute, Colombo, 1994.

Soesatro, Hadi, "Implications of the Post-Cold War Politico-Security Environment on the Pacific Economy" in Pacific Dynamism and the International Economic System (ed.) by C. Fred Bergsten and Marcus Noland, Washington D.C., 1993.

Stockwin, Harvey, "APEC without India: But All is Not Lost", *The Times of India*, 20th November, 1994.

Yoo, Jang-Hee, "A Future Perspective of APEC", *Asian Economic Journal*, Vol. 9, No. 1, 1995.

6

India and Indian Ocean Rim Association (IORA)

Indian Ocean Rim Association (IORA)—formerly called Indian Ocean Rim Association for Regional Cooperation (IOR-ARC)—of which India is a member, came into existence in March 1997 after initial meetings, called the "Mauritius Initiative". It initially consisted of fourteen countries viz., Australia, India, Indonesia, Kenya, Madagascar, Malaysia, Mauritius, Mozambique, Oman, Singapore, South Africa, Sri Lanka, Tanzania and Yemen. At the second meeting of the Council of Ministers of the IOR-ARC in Maputo, Mozambique in March 1999, it was decided to admit five more members: Bangladesh, Iran, Seychelles, Thailand and the United Arab Emirates. Union of Comoros was inducted as the twentieth member on November 2, 2012. The Council of Ministers (COM) is the apex body of IORA; besides there are two other bodies—IORBF (Indian Ocean Rim Business Forum) and IORAG (Indian Ocean Rim Academic Group). (These come under what is called the non-governmental Track-2 initiatives).

It is claimed that IORA has enormous economic potential and offers considerable trade and investment opportunities. South Africa is rich in minerals and is a major economic power in Africa. East Africa has enormous tourist potential. South Asia has abundant skilled manpower and untapped markets. Southeast Asia is an economic powerhouse, and Australia is rich in natural resources and a developed country. However, it must be remembered that the Indian Ocean Region comprises a collection of economically diverse and disparate countries. It is characterized by significant variations in levels of wealth and economic development, economic and trade interests, including dependence on regional trade, and political interest in regional cooperation.

Australia, Singapore and United Arab Emirates fall in the

high-income category. Malaysia, Mauritius, Oman, Seychelles and South Africa are in the upper middle-income category. Indonesia, Iran, Sri Lanka and Thailand fall in the lower middle-income category. Finally, Bangladesh, India, Kenya, Madagascar, Mozambique, Tanzania and Yemen belong to the low-income category. These low-income countries, with the exception of India and Kenya are among the least developed countries of the world. A country like Mozambique with one of the lowest per capita incomes in the world has little in common with a high growth country like Singapore.

IORA member countries actively participate in the global trading environment at the commercial and political level. Exports from IORA countries to all markets grew almost 500 percent in the 1990s, almost six times their previous level, but Singapore-Malaysia trade dominates IORA trade. IORA controls only 10.7 percent of the world trade, and intra-regional trade amounts to 25 percent, and thus it is not in a position to dominate global trade liberalization. There is little potential for member countries of the Indian Ocean region to deepen economic linkages and increase trade and investment flows. Studies show that trade increases were not linked to the formation of the IORA.

Approaches to regional cooperation will therefore be heavily influenced by these considerations.

The history of regional cooperation suggests that regional arrangements involve a dynamic process, often developing from relatively modest proposals, when compared with their subsequent evolution. This has been the case with the European Union (EU) and the North American Free Trade Area (NAFTA).

Regional arrangements vary in their scope and depth of integration. At one extreme, they may be no more than informal consultative forums. More advanced, yet still shallow, forms of integration involve preferential trading arrangements, which extend lower tariff preferences to members than to non-members. Preferential arrangements may also include agreements on investments, standards and other regulatory issues.

Deeper forms of integration involve the formation of a single economics area behind common external tariffs. Such arrangements may extend to national governments ceding trade policy to a supra-national body, and pursuing the harmonisation of their micro and macro policies. The European Union (EU) is such a type of regional organization.

Regional arrangements may be driven either by market or political imperatives, or more usually some combination of both. All regional arrangements and other forms of regional cooperation can be positioned along a continuum from market driven to a politically driven integration. At the far market driven end, would be integration in the South China Region (Guangdong, Fujian, Taiwan and Hong Kong), where the economies of Taiwan and the Mainland, do not recognise each other politically. At the far end of the policy driven arrangements, with little market basis to integration, are many of the formal economic arrangements in Latin America and Africa in the 1960s and 1970s.

The IORA is based on the concept of open regionalism, which is distinct from preferential regionalism. In preferential regionalism, trade preferences are given to members at reduced tariffs. This results in a net positive impact on trade among members. It may also have a negative impact or no effect on trade with non-members due to trade diversion. Regional co-operation, which promotes the benefits of closer regional ties, but without any discriminatory trade measures, is open regionalism. Simply put, open regionalism is trade liberalisation among the member countries in the region on a most favoured nation (MFN) basis unilaterally, without asking for reciprocity from non-members.

It is argued that open regionalism is a flexible arrangement that is more member friendly than neo-liberalist regional arrangements such as preferential trading arrangements, free trade areas etc. There are no laws and binding contracts and decisions are made by consensus. Compliance to any commitment is voluntary and there is no rigid institutional structure and bureaucratic set up to specify obligations.

Integration of the IOR will depend on the complementarity—in terms of resources, skills, markets, investment flows of the countries of the region, and policy reforms (particularly domestic economic reform policies), that provide trade and investment opportunities. There are no binding contracts, and decisions are made by consensus. There is considerable confusion about the implications and relevance of open regionalism. The logic of the case of economic benefits to be won by unilateral liberalization is weak. There is always reluctance to comprehensive reduction of trade barriers. With unstructured arrangements, coordination is limited. A dialogue-oriented forum will not be as successful in economic terms as an action-oriented regional bloc will. Project driven confidence-building measures will not be sufficient to sustain a regional grouping.

The basic ingredients for effective market integration to support open regionalism are not in place in the IORA. Only that part of the IORA that has strongly benefited from FDI is the Southeast Asia sub-region and to a lesser extent Australia. The analysis of trade flow statistics shows that the expected spin-off of accelerated economic growth in these regions has not permeated the larger region.

In the current IORA agenda, there are projects under various working groups. Some of them have made considerable progress and reached a stage of recommending various sector-related policy proposals. These projects can be categorised into two broad areas: (a) trade and investment facilitation, and (b) economic and technical co-operation. The projects are on standards and accreditation, investment facilitation and promotion, trade promotion, improvement in maritime transport, human resource development, tourism promotion and development. The follow up on projects has been very tardy.

IOR covers too many individual countries, with significant differences in factor endowments. Similar economic structures mean limited trade opportunities. There are also limited complementarities in terms of savings—most of the economies are borrowers—and in terms of supply and demand for advanced capital goods and technology.

Almost 90 percent of intra-IORA trade and its growth come from the Southeast Asian countries. North and East African and Indian Ocean Island sub-groups have contributed only marginally to intra-IORA trade and its growth. The analysis of trade flow statistics shows that the expected spin-off of accelerated economic growth in these regions has not permeated to the larger region.

The Indian Ocean group is much too disparate and scattered to make a mark in the near future. South Africa has its own African commitments, has a sagging interest in IORA and is overburdened by regional pulls in its immediate neighbourhood. There are renewed financial problems in Southeast Asia, and the economies have once again slowed down, after recovering from the financial crisis of 1997. Australia has a reluctant "look west" policy, and continues her close ties with the Pacific, particularly the United States.

Moreover, Australia was interested in the IORA, more from a security/defence perspective rather than economic cooperation. Mauritius and Oman are active in the IORA, because they need more economic space to assert themselves. Mauritius is better known for routing questionable foreign investment through its shores to India—known as the "Mauritius Route". In any case such grandiose schemes of regional cooperation spanning three Continents, from Canberra to Cape Town, with Kolkata along the way are far too ambitious to be economically viable.

The influence of the Indian Diaspora in promoting intra-IORA trade and directing it to India has also been minimal, unlike the Chinese and their strong GUANXI (networking contracts) with a lasting contribution to the development of Mainland China. Compliance to any commitment is voluntary and there is no rigid institutional structure to enforce obligations.

As regards the so-called Track2 initiatives, the IORAG

also has not contributed much to furthering Rim cooperation.

Bilateral initiatives will yield greater flows of trade, than over-ambitious regional cooperation plans. To increase India's share of merchandise exports from the stagnant 0.7 percent to a higher level, sustained export promotion should be the constant endeavour of the government. These should include reduction in transaction costs through decentralisation, simplification of procedures, and identification of thrust sectors. Measures such as special economic zones, promotion of agricultural exports, market access initiatives, setting up business cum trade facilitation centres/trade portals and duty free replenishments, should be pursued with renewed vigour. India should further intensify her trade with the European Union and select ASEAN countries like Malaysia and Singapore, where there are new opportunities emerging in the post-WTO accord world. Bilateral free trade pacts like India has with Nepal and Sri Lanka should be encouraged.

Thus, India should focus her economic diplomacy on deepening bilateral engagement and FTAs (free trade agreements) rather than in pursuing regional cooperation with an amorphous and heterogeneous group of countries, like in the Indian Ocean region.

7

India and the European Union (EU)

The European Union (EU) today is the world's most successful regional organization, accounting for 63 percent of total bloc exports. Intra-bloc exports in SAARC, (South Asia Association for Regional Cooperation) with India as a member, are still only 5 percent. The EU has shown much more commitment than any other regional organization. It has aspects of both supra-nationalism and inter-governmentalism. India also has many similarities with EU. EU's development has transformed governance in Europe, influencing everything from regulations on the habitat of birds, to voting in WTO. It has also altered global politics, governance and the relationship of nation-states in the post-Cold War era. There is nevertheless a "democratic deficit" in Europe. Decisions are made by governmental leaders and bureaucrats without direct input from voters. In India too, "democracy" means periodic elections, which bring about a "compromise between competing elites", and without altering the basic conditions of the poverty-ridden masses.

India and the EU are the two largest democracies in the world, sharing a common bond of pluralism, consultation, consensus, and rule of law, strength of democratic institutions, a strong and free press, and an independent judiciary. These are the principal features defining their strategic partnership. These principles help manage their continental-sized polities and economies. Decision-making structures are federative, inclusive, caring and conciliatory.

India and the EU are the foremost examples of multiculturalism, that countries elsewhere in the world must embrace as an inevitable consequences of globalization, and the new world order. India views the EU as an independent and indispensable pillar of a world edifice resting on multiple pillars, capable of making significant contributions towards fostering a rule-based international order, and in coming to terms with the challenges of managing global interdependence. The EU is one of India's largest trading partner and source of foreign direct investment (FDI). Our economic partnership is based on firm foundations. Indian companies are investing in sectors as diverse as IT (information technology), bio-technology, food processing, automotive components, and pharmaceuticals.

India sees EU as a natural partner in its economic development, and interaction with the rest of the world. The strategic partnership is no longer economic-driven, but covers diverse areas of engagement. We share a mutuality of interests on many global issues. We are partners in an intensified fight against terrorism, nuclear proliferation, unsustainable environment, and sectarian conflict. When the EU, the world's biggest trading bloc and the largest integrated single market economy co-operates with India—the second most populous nation and the fourth largest, fast growing economy—the significance of the partnership goes beyond bilateral relations and impacts on global equations.

The EU sees Indian multiculturalism and its apparent success, as an example where one can learn from each other's experience. In EU circles, it is felt if India can exist as a mosaic of ethnicities, religions, languages and cultures, why can't Europe follow the same path?

At the superficial level, there are plenty of similarities between the EU and India. The EU comprises 28 nations with more queuing up. India has 29 states, each marked by distinctive culture, and 18 official languages. Christianity is the primary religion in Europe: Hinduism in India. Both EU and India have significant minority populations. But, of course, there are profound differences too. Europe after all is the cradle of modern nationalism, and some members of the EU are the oldest nation-states in the world. Thus, however much the EU tries to gloss over angularities of nationalism; it continues to stumble on them.

What the claim to equate EU with India does is to posit civilizational basis for Europe. The problem with this formulation came to the fore when both France and the Netherlands rejected the European constitution. An important reason for this is strong nationalist sentiments in both countries, as opposed to pan-European identities. The attitude to particular religious minority—Muslims—in Europe brings to the fore EU's policy of multicultural harmonization. As a greater number of Muslims, many of them belonging to a generation raised and nurtured in Europe are implicated in terrorist acts. EU member-states policies towards minorities and migration are being severely tested. The role of the State should be clearly defined—does the State impose hard secularism and uniform citizenship on its citizens as in France, or does it give more play to multiple notions of identity? Many of these concerns, especially with regard to EU's expansion plans come into focus when the question of Turkey's entry to the EU crops up.

India's problems are similar to EU's in many aspects. Despite the success of India's multiculturalism, there are serious flaws in the ways it is formulated and practised in India. Though the Indian State has been vociferous in its defence of multiculturalism, it has often failed to deliver. The Constitution of India has clauses that contain aspects of Hindu majoritarianism, despite India's professed multiculturalism, and secular credentials. The State's and judiciary's construction of Hinduism is intent on homogeneity. The wording of the Constitution is also instructive. The reference to Hindus in Article 25 includes Sikhs, Jains and Buddhists. It is not only the State that makes a mockery of the slogan, "Unity in Diversity". For most Indians, diversity is something that is best celebrated in theory. As soon as diversity threatens the majority, it falls back on uniformity and national unity, for "survival of the Nation".

Economic co-operation between India and Europe is

gathering momentum. India-EU bilateral trade has grown from € 28.6 billion in 2003 to €72.7 billion in 2013. EU is a major source of high grade technology and technology transfer. Indo-German collaboration companies were market leaders in as many as 15 product groups.

However, the European economies have not been able to take full advantage of the expansion of the Indian economy. One of the reasons for this is the slow growth of the European economies—less than 2.5 percent decadal growth.

As economic growth in the EU is projected to rebound in the coming years, this is the appropriate time to give a boost to India-EU economic cooperation.

Indo-EU ties are now upgraded to a "strategic partnership", after the annual summits since 2000, covering all aspects of economic and political cooperation.

Movement of professionals between EU and India should be possible with the mutual recognition of higher qualifications.

With a special relationship, Indian companies can penetrate in a big way rapidly growing European outsourcing. Integration of economies would improve the competitiveness of both India and the EU.

A rapidly aging population coupled with increasingly better standards of living amongst EU citizens has prompted the EU to look towards Asia to bridge labour-supply gaps.

Europe is today a global super power of world historical importance, second to none in economic clout. It has constructed one of the most successful systems of government —the modern social welfare state—which for all its flaws has brought in unprecedented prosperity and security to Europe's people. It is the single most successful contributor to voluntary international cooperation.

The original European Economic Community (ECC) of 1957 has grown from the founding six members to 28, knitting together 503 million people. Its values are spreading across the globe—far more attractive, in many respects, than those of

America. Europe's trajectory is up, not down, and is even rising.

Northern Europe's social democracies are on top of the World Economic Forum's ranking of the most competitive economies. 60 percent of US foreign investment goes to Europe. US business invests more in European nations like Belgium, Ireland, and Switzerland than in the whole of China or India. Instruments to engineer peace, the softer tools of civilian power, lie with Europe—the "quiet super power".

EU has emerged as Europe's most innovative and significant contribution to modernity. Europe and EU emphasizes community relationships over individual autonomy, cultural diversity over assimilation, quality of life over accumulation of wealth, sustainable development over unlimited material growth, deep play over unrelenting toil, and universal human rights, India too values all these qualities. Hence, we should work together to harmonize our synergies, through closer collaboration and interaction.

It is only through multiculturalism shared by both India and the EU that global problems such as terrorism, environmental degradation, reviving WTO talks and religious fundamentalism can be mitigated.

The Berlin Declaration, commemorating EU at 50 states, "for centuries Europe has been an idea, holding out hope of peace and understanding. That hope has been fulfilled". The real success of both India and the EU are linguistic pluralism, accommodation of diversities and heterogeneities and above all functioning of vibrant parliamentary democracies.

The commonality of values between India and the EU, pluralism, consultation, strength of democratic institutions, independent judiciary and free press, are part of the mutuality of interests. India and the European Union are the two foremost examples of multiculturalism and plurality of identities, something that countries in other continents must embrace as an inevitable aspect and consequence of globalization. Despite the flaws of multiculturalism, India and the EU see each other as indispensable pillars, making significant contributions towards fostering a rule-based international order and in meeting the challenges of global reciprocity and independence.

The forerunner of the European Union (EU) was the European Coal and Steel Community, established in the early 1950s. This evolved into the European Economic Community (EEC) also known as the European Common Market (ECM) or the European Community (EC), and now as the European Union (EU). It is the most successful of regional economic integration schemes.

The EEC, originally comprised six nations—Belgium, France, Federal Republic of Germany, Italy, Luxembourg and the Netherlands—came into being on January 1, 1958 by the virtue of the Treaty of Rome of 1957. The EEC was expanded in 1973, with the inclusion of the UK, Denmark and Ireland. Greece joined the community in 1981, Spain and Portugal became members in 1986. Austria, Finland and Sweden also joined the EC later with the membership rising to 15. Today, the EU has 28 members, including some countries, of the former Soviet Bloc in Eastern Europe, and some of the newly liberated countries of the former Soviet Union.

The objectives of the formation of the EU as envisaged in the Treaty of Rome are:

1. Elimination of tariffs, quotas and other barriers on intra-community trade,
2. Having a common internal tariff on imports from the rest of the world,
3. Allowing the free movement of factors of production within the community,
4. Harmonization of taxation and monetary policies and also social security policies, and
5. Adopting a common policy on agriculture, transport and competition in industry.

The EU, taken as a single unit is one of India's largest trading partner. India's main exports to the EU include textiles, jute, leather and leather goods, and polished diamonds engineering goods, chemicals, and marine products. Imports include edible oils, fertilizers, dairy products, steel, capital goods, optical instruments, alumina and copper products, synthetic rubber, photo and cinema equipment. India also receives technology investment and development from the EU countries.

India's export performance to EU has been marred with certain factors which include lack of price competitiveness, poor quality, poor reputation with respect to delivery schedules, inadequate export marketing skills, and protectionist policies of the EU countries. These factors have contributed to a sluggish growth in India-EU trade, particularly India's exports to EU. India should pay great attention to the emerging opportunities in the EU, and improve quality of exports and stick to delivery schedules.

8

Sino-Indian Economic Relations

India is a vibrant democracy, despite vast religious, caste and economic diversities. China's per capita income began to exceed India's in the 1990s, though forty years earlier, India's was above that of China. India had avoided the pitfalls of the Great Leap Forward and the Cultural Revolution, though after the Reforms of Deng Xiao Ping since 1978, China is way ahead of India in all the economic and social parameters. In 1991, the Indian government initiated economic reforms. India's market-oriented liberalization and removal of industrial licensing and controls resulted in acceleration of GDP to about 6 percent a year since 1991, among the fastest for any nation, but considerably lower than the Chinese pace of about 9 percent for the corresponding period.

China's amazing economic success is stunning the world, and China understands how to move with the times like no other country. Its aim is to be a middle-level developed country in the mid-twenty first century. China is the world's most competitive nation, and was the largest exporter in 2013 with exports valued at US$ 1.90 trillion. China desires to modernize rapidly by attracting more foreign investment. However, it must be remembered that the share of FDI in total investment in China is less than 8 percent, reflecting the extent of capital formation in the economy. The entry of China into the WTO will make China a more transparent and less subsidized economy, meaning more market access opportunity in the domestic markets of China. India could be described until recently as a traditional "mixed economy" with a large public sector, but also a lot of private entrepreneurship.

China's Economy: Small Steps to Giant Leaps

China has been on a high growth trajectory for more than

three decades, while even maintaining a sustainable rate of growth at more than 9 percent per annum during the period 2002-10. The rate of domestic expansion has been robust since its accession to the WTO in 2001. As is evident from statistics, the main drivers of China's economic growth have been its exports and a subsequent expansion of the domestic sector, accompanied by its import surge. During 2012, China's export share in the world economy stood at 11.13 percent, and the corresponding share for its imports was 9.77 percent.

The global economy started recovering from recession in 2010, but with the deepening of the financial situation in Europe once again entered the danger zone until the third quarter of 2012. However, the U.S. economy has shown positive forward movements in GDP growth and a persistent development in the employment situation in 2012 (IMF, 2012b). The global situation continued to remain fragile in 2012, and its adverse impact was felt in most of the emerging countries that included China and India. Though it suffered from global downturn, China has been strategizing to take advantage from the expected recovery of the global economy.

China by contrast has been for the most part a command economy, which until recently had a small private sector, and only recognized the legal possibility of home-grown capitalists a few years ago. The Chinese economy has grown at an average annual rate of 9.8 percent for two-and-half decades, while India's economy has grown at around 5-6 percent per year over the same period. Chinese growth has been relatively volatile around this trend, reflecting stop-go-cycles of state response to inflation through aggregate credit management. The higher growth in China essentially occurs because of the much higher rate of investment in China. The investment rate in China (investment as a share of GDP) has fluctuated between 35 to 44 percent over the past 25 years, compared to 20 percent to 26 percent in India. In fact, the aggregate incremental capital-output ratios (ICORs) have been around the same in both economies. Within this, there is the critical role of infrastructure investment, which has averaged at 19 percent of GDP in China compared to 2 percent in India over the 1990s.

Trends in Chinese Trade with the World

In the resurgence of the Chinese economy in the recent decade, the external sector played an important role, though it passed through a phase of volatility due to the periodic swings of global business cycle. Between 1998 and 2009, reflecting the periods of recovery from global recession, Chinese trade with the world economy registered a seven-fold increase, surpassing the performances of other fast growing countries of the world. Total export was US$ 184 billion in 1998 and increased to US$ 1.2 trillion in 2009. Similarly, imports increased from US$ 140 billion to one trillion dollar between 1998 and 2009, showing a more than seven-fold increase during the decade. It is important to note that imports increased more rapidly than exports.

The mantra of China is sharply focused on becoming an economic superpower and hence everything else follows—foreign policy begins and ends with economic policy. China is creating a national economy, and the result is a massive and painful restructuring of industry and society. Competition across provincial boundaries is becoming a reality. As a result, the country is experiencing deflation, a continual decline in prices. As prices fall, the economy stagnates.

Chinese export growth has been much more rapid, involving aggressive increases in world market shares. This export growth has been based on relocative capital that has been attracted not only by cheap labour but also by excellent and heavily subsidized infrastructure, resulting from the high rate of infrastructure investment. In addition, since the Chinese state has also been keen on provision of basic goods in terms of housing, food and cheap transport facilities, this has played an important role in reducing labour costs for employers. In India, the cheap labour has been because of low absolute wages rather than public provision and underwriting of labour costs, and infrastructure development has been minimal. So it is not surprising that it has not really been an attractive location for export-oriented investment, its rate of export growth has been much lower, and exports have not become an engine of growth.

In terms of inequality, in both economies the recent pattern of growth has been inequitable. In China, the spatial inequalities across regions have been the sharpest. In India, vertical inequalities and rural-urban divide have become much more marked.

In China, recently as a response to this, there have been some top-down measures to reduce inequality, for example through changes in tax rates, greater public investment in western and interior regions and improved social security benefits. In India, it is political change that has forced greater attention to redressing inequalities, though the process is still very incipient.

In terms of the future prospects, surprisingly, both economies end up with very similar issues despite these major differences. There are clear questions of sustainability of the current pattern of economic expansion in China, based on high export-accumulation model that requires constantly increasing shares in world markets and very high investment rates. Similarly, the hope in some policy quarters in India that information technology-enabled services can become the engine of growth, raises the problems of sustainability.

The most important problems in the two economies are also similar mainly the agrarian crisis and the need to generate more employment. In both economies, the social sectors have been neglected recently by public intervention. In both countries, the policy message appears to be the same, that the most basic issues are those that require to be addressed first, and if so, the other areas of expansion will probably look after themselves.

Democracy, Communism and Economic Restrictions

India has individual liberty, political pluralism, and the institutional framework to take advantage of globalization. However, it is constrained by mass poverty, lackadaisical government, growing fiscal problems, and a poor physical infrastructure. China has much less degrading poverty than India, which has more trade and investment links, while Chinese have a superior physical infrastructure. It is rapidly conforming to global behaviour patterns, and creating an internationally accepted legal system. However, it too has fiscal problems, the banking system, and political risk.

China's industrial strength and infrastructure, and its vast pool of skilled labour, make it a natural choice for the manufacturing sector. India, on the other hand, with booming information technology sector and its huge reserves of English speaking graduates, is a better option for outsourced service and technology development facilities. China has been favoured heavily by multinational corporations (MNCs) for manufacturing, with only limited business process outsourcing (BPO) activity coming in from Japanese and Korean firms. As opposed to the concentrated outsourced services and R&D facilities found in India, China is the hub of manufacturing.

As the WTO and TRIPS agreements progress, the export orientation of each country may cross into the present domain of the other due to drops in garment quota requirements and strengthening of the IPR culture

The key strategies of Chinese reforms was to first effect a massive increase in incomes in the rural areas, and then meet the demand for consumer goods by encouraging the growth of VTEs (village and town enterprises). The VTEs met the demand for basic consumer goods in the rural areas itself. There was continuous decentralization, and a system of profit taking with punishment for default. In India, the agricultural sector still accounts for about 70 percent of employment, but its share in GDP was down to 12 percent in 2012-2013; in other words the relative per capita income of the agricultural worker is down.

China can assist India in her globalization efforts, by cheaper imports from China and using them to produce low cost products in India itself, through the joint-venture strategy. By trading with China, India can be a little more competitive in global markets. A strategy of engagement with China and facing up to competition can be India's policy for the future.

India must emulate China by taking advantage of its cheap, hardworking and skilled workers to leverage better in world markets. To compete effectively, India needs to expand its primary and secondary education, and give more emphasis to vocational education and training.

China is in fact "*many small markets*", rather than "*the world's biggest market*". China today has good infrastructure—railways, roads and airports—so there is for the first time, substantial inter-city and inter-provincial commerce, as one city can compete against "backward manufacturers" in another. Consequently, there is the rise of national domestic brands.

At the political level, the Communist Party of China, eaten underneath by corruption still survives. One day new attitudes will push aside the corruption of the old, and a new China will emerge. Beijing strikes hard against recalcitrant elements and dissidents—but dissidents can be muzzled—not their ideas.

Since 1978, when the great modernizer, Deng Xiao Ping began China's reforms, and later in the nineties with former President's Jiang Zemin's vision, China has moved rapidly in its growth rates. However, the new Chinese leadership needs to move ahead faster in political reforms. To recall, Chairman Mao's words "*it takes only one spark to start a prairie fire*". The next spark should not cause any dramatic upheavals.

The share of manufacturing in China's GDP in 2013 was 43.9 percent, and services constituted 46.1 percent of the GDP. The biggest current draw for international investors is the "*Western Development Project*" (headquarters in Chonqing), initiating grandiose plans for Xinjiang and Tibet.

At the geo-political level, Sino-Indian relations should rise above the present border disputes, and past tilts. Relations should be non-hyphenated, and stand-alone, not guided by any third country. India occupies a special place, as the land of the Buddha in China. There is also admiration in India for China's economic achievements. India has an edge over China in terms of intellectual capital for the future knowledge economy. Some of the general strengths and weaknesses of India and China are enumerated below.

Strengths and Weaknesses of China

Strengths of China

- Confucian ethic of discipline and obedience.
- Authoritarian militarist state, with severe penalties for non-compliance.
- Highly disciplined top leadership that implements decisions once agreed, without further argument.
- Productivity of Chinese labour is five times that of India.
- China has a system of incentives and disincentives at central, state and town-level for performance.
- Small-scale imitator of well-known brands, giving better quality for a lesser price, not the original branded manufacturer. Chinese "under design" products to make them affordable by poorer households. Those who can afford to pay more for superior quality do so. In India, established manufacturers are unlike the Chinese; they are conditioned by MNCs, whose practices evolved in markets that can afford high prices for superior products, and that suited an economy where capacities were restricted by license. China dominates export of labour-intensive products world wide; India does not, except in gems and jewellery.
- China has a system of incentives and disincentives at central, state and town-level for performance and non-performance.
- Foreign investment in China is in land, buildings, plant and machinery. Of the comparatively small foreign

investment in India, a high proportion is in portfolio investment, and in buying existing capacities.

Weaknesses of China

- Communist Party of China still dominating, with no democratic dissent tolerated.
- The Chinese legal system has still many weaknesses for corporate grievance redressal.
- China is yet to adapt fully to rules and regulations of a free market economy.
- China has lax labour regulations, and workers in many industries have to toil for longer hours.
- Working conditions are tough, as workers stay in crammed dormitories inside industrial zones to work from 8 a.m. to 8 p.m. They are not allowed to form their own associations at national or regional level. This advantage may not last long, as workers become conscious of their rights. Even though labour issues are not raised at WTO, such unsound procedures and practices could come under attack.
- China's entry into WTO will call for a "fresh look" at its global interaction and domestic re-structuring.
- Corporate governance too is not of a high quality, as transactions are not wholly transparent. Managers of state enterprises indulge in various irregularities, like siphoning of funds offshore, which in many cases comes back disguised as FDI.
- Chinese capital markets too are relatively underdeveloped—regulations are not in tune with free-market earnings.

Strengths and Weaknesses of India

Strengths of India

- A stable and vibrant democracy. *India's greatest achievement is sustaining a democracy in exceptionally difficult circumstances.*
- Wide use of the English Language.
- Availability of world-class scientific, technical, managerial

and professional manpower.

- Established Western style corporate democracy and a functioning legal system for grievance redressal and contract enforcement.
- A growing and sizable middle-class estimated at 300 million.
- Our culture encourages risk without reward, and as our defence forces have shown, we can be extremely disciplined and productive.

Weaknesses of India

- Hypocrisy of our political leadership.
- Poor implementation capacity of our administration.
- Speculative mentality of our industry.
- Rampant corruption, stifling the delivery system of any constructive programme.
- *"Vested interests" and "entrenched rural hierarchies" hampering any societal changes.*
- Our bureaucrats and politicians have yet to develop awareness that more trade and intensified economic relations enhances India's security, power and influence.

The similarities are striking. China and India are amongst the five biggest countries in the world in terms of area, geographical diversity, population, market size and economy measured in terms of purchasing power parity. Both countries were colonized by western powers, and attained independence within a few years of each other in the mid-twentieth century. They both pursued socialist models of development before opening up gradually, China from 1978, and India from 1991. China and India are presently the fastest growing major economies of the world, although the majority of the population continues to be dependent on agriculture. The state sector continues to dominate economic activity in both countries, with the role of private enterprise expanding fast. In both China and India rapid economic growth has widened regional economic disparities.

Issues of Mutual Concern

Both China and India face serious fiscal problems and ballooning domestic debt and contingent liabilities, needing major public sector adjustments in the foreseeable future. However, much of India's public sector deficit has been absorbed directly by the government, whereas China has relied more heavily on the banking system to fund the deficit. Therefore, while India has higher fiscal deficits, China's banking system has more non-performing assets.

Corruption is endemic in both China and India. However, in China it is more centralized around the entrenched communist party, which practically guarantees quick action. In India corruption is more dispersed, and outcomes less certain. Because corruption in India is subject to legislative, media and judicial oversight, it is less of a systemic risk than in China.

China has shown far grater urgency in privatizing and closing a large number of state enterprises, while India's privatization programme has floundered. While China has effectively lowered trade barriers, with customs tariff collections comprising only about 3 percent ad valorem, Indian tariffs are still amongst the world's highest. Economic decentralization has proceeded at a much faster pace in China, with local governments in China having effective economic strengths and decision-making powers; whereas India's centralized economic control is loosening only gradually.

While China is a closed society run by a tightly knit communist party, India is an open, democratic society, with an independent judiciary and press. With political dissent not aired in the public domain, China has overt political stability, arguably difficult to sustain during a severe economic downswing.

Both China and India face major future developmental threats: for India these centre on policies to enhance savings and growth rates to remove poverty within a targeted time frame; for China the threats are more institutional, with institutions, especially financial, legal and political, not in sync with the needs of a market economy. In the pre-accession period, the Chinese economy was passing through a phase of rapid economic transition.

Economic Environment in China

The macro economic reforms undertaken by China, including its trade reforms, industrial policy changes, investment liberalization, and other macroeconomic restructuring have contributed to a positive overall performance of its economy. Some of these initiatives are discussed below.

After 15 years of negotiations for entry into the WTO, China's accession to the same in 2001 was a major development in its trade policy. Many analysts in China and abroad believe that the terms of agreement were quite tough on China in many areas, such as the financial sector where China agreed to liberalise more than what it obtained from some developed countries. China's post-WTO accession tariff rates are 'bound', meaning that China cannot raise them above the bound rates without 'compensating' the WTO trading partners. All these have drastically reduced China's 'policy space' for active development policy.

Despite these concessions, China would not be given the status of a market economy until 2016, which means that until that date importing countries would bring in anti-dumping actions without having to prove that the export prices were lower than the domestic market prices in exporting countries. Instead, costs in a third country can be used to measure the so-called 'normal value' for anti-dumping action. The process is thus open to somewhat arbitrary action and it is no wonder that China has become the target of the largest number of anti-dumping cases for several years in a row. Obtaining market economy status features prominently in China's bilateral trade agreements. A perception of an unfair agreement under WTO accession prevails in many trade policy quarters in China.

China has also reluctantly accepted some discriminatory

provisions in its accession protocol which can be used to limit access of its exports to overseas markets. The first is the transitional product-specific safeguard mechanism which targets Chinese products. It can be invoked if there is market disruption or the threat of market disruption caused by Chinese imports, instead of a more stringent injury test under the WTO Agreement on Safeguards. This safeguard mechanism will last for 12 years after China's accession to the WTO. The second is the special safeguard mechanism which was applicable to China's textile and clothing exports until the end of 2008. It provides for a 6 to 7.5 percent annual increase in the growth of Chinese exports and it can be invoked immediately upon request by the importing country for consultation with China. An implication of the latter is that China has been restrained from taking full advantage of the MFA phase-out under the Agreement on Textiles and Clothing until the end of 2008.

India's Exports to China: Constraints

In general, tariffs in China are lower than those in India particularly, for India's major export items such as ores, pharmaceutical products, plastics, manmade staple fibers, and iron and steel. The non-tariff barriers and informal restrictions are of greater concern. Such restrictions in China on imports of goods and services apply to imports from India as well. Indian industry and business organizations have identified similar constraints in promoting their exports to China, for example, customs procedures, standards, certification and regulatory practices, and quantitative restrictions.

It was noted while examining the customs procedures that even after the issuance of valuation regulations in accordance with WTO Customs Valuation Agreement, many customs officials continue to use the minimum or reference price rather than the actual transaction price for valuation of goods. The same product may be subject to a case-by-case determination of customs value depending on the port of entry and often the decision regarding duty on the products becomes a subject of negotiations between traders and customs officials. Re-exporters are allowed to import raw material only through a specified port. If they operate through other ports, they have to follow extremely difficult procedures to avail of duty free clearance of cargo. This problem is especially serious for Indian traders because of the limited transport links between India and China, which do not allow free choice of ports for landing.

Rules and regulations pertaining to standards and certification as applied to imports are different from those applied to domestic goods and these are frequently changed, the details of which are not easily available in a published form in the English language. The implementation of these regulations is different at different levels of government, with very little coordination between national and sub-national levels. Exemption procedures for import of replacement parts or imports of parts for assembly and re-export are burdensome and costly as the application is to be submitted in person and requires knowledge of the local language. Certification remains difficult, time consuming and a costly process for many commodities, of interest to Indian exporters,

Recent Trends in Bilateral Trade

The Sino-Indian bilateral trade relationship took an impressive turn during the last decade as China gradually ascended to become the largest trading partner of India since 2008. Bilateral two-way trade jumped by nearly twelve and a half times during the period 2000-10 and total trade is expected to reach the level of nearly US$ 100 billion by the end of 2015. During the last decade, exports of India to China grew at the rate of 39.0 percent per annum, and formed nearly 8.0 percent of the total exports of India in 2010. During global recession, India's bilateral imports expanded faster than the bilateral exports. With an increase in two-way trade, the trade deficit increased exponentially, and bilateral trade imbalance caused concern about the sustainability of rising bilateral trade over a time. However, both countries have aimed at achieving the trade target of US$ 100 billion by 2015.

As external sector is turning to be a major driver of growth during the last decade, both the economies have been dealing with appropriate development strategies to keep their economies on high growth trajectory. Deliberate policy interventions have been experimented systematically to insulate these economies from the vagaries of intermittent global shocks and mitigating challenges of being middle-income country. Both the countries have resorted to rapid trade liberalization, mostly induced by unilateral initiative to cope with the global trading environment. Both countries witness regional disparity in having access to international trade and this development gap could provide an opportunity to augment bilateral trade between them. India has a large export potential in China, and it could emerge as a competitive supplier in the Chinese market, based on its global competitiveness. India is yet to introduce a number of products, which are globally competitive in the Chinese market.

Having a large domestic market in value chain in a number of sectors, including the parts and component sector, India can complement China as an efficient partner in this sector and could be more competitive than several Southeast Asian economies upon whom China is seriously dependent for intermediate input supplies. Moreover, undervaluation of renminbi has posed certain amount of threat to India where both counties are competing for market access for same set of products. Revaluation of renminbi could improve India's export prospects in some sectors if not all. Both countries can play a constructive role in the regional integration process in East Asia. EAS process is marred by the Chinese stand on ASEAN-Plus Three (APT), but realization of Regional Comprehensive Economic Partnership (RCEP) (which was known as EAS earlier) could steer the region on a high growth track, and China is likely to benefit more than what is expected from the APT process.

Both China and India are of the view that regionalism can

offer a credible platform to augment regional trade. As their trade is mostly concentrated in Asia, particularly in Southeast and East Asia, this trade area is becoming important for accessing the regional market.

China could overtake India as the next information technology (IT) power and business-outsourcing hub for countries like the US, despite its lack of experience. China's offshore services will mature within the next five years, and companies should begin looking at the country as a potential source for IT-enabled services. Lower costs (roughly 1/6th of US counterparts), political stability, strong GDP growth (7.9 percent in 2001)—the country offers the kind of environment needed by interested global companies.

Looking at India-China bilateral trade composition-wise, India's top five exports to China comprise mainly primary or low value-addition products viz. iron ore, plastic and linoleum, ores and minerals, marine products and drugs and pharmaceuticals. Her imports from China are electronic goods, coal, coke, and organic chemicals, silk, medicinal and pharmaceutical products. India should move up the value chain, and export more IT-related products and pharmaceuticals, as it is doing recently.

However, despite China's better image abroad, the image of Indians abroad is also very high and has been improving. The Indian Diaspora has gained considerable mileage abroad, the number of Indian $ billionaires live in the US and are highly rated. Despite loud proclamations, foreign investors consider everything unfriendly about India—the government, the bureaucracy and the infrastructure. We have to change the mind-set and working of Indian institutions.

India's trade with China is set to grow to US$ 100 billion by 2015. If the trade and economic linkages is to expand exponentially, it is imperative that diversification takes place in the commodity-mix. China and India between themselves produce practically everything, cheaply and with high quality. With high export growth rates, India and China are galloping, but they must also gallop in tandem with each other.

A recent study by Goldman Sachs shows that India will take a long time to catch up with China—may not catch up even by 2050. This is because China has a much larger base in GDP than India; therefore, even a smaller relative increase in income for China would mean a higher absolute increase than India. This is shown in Table 8.1.

Table 8.1: What Will it Take for India to Catch up with China?

India	Year	Growth Rate (percent)
To catch up China by	2050	8.9
To catch up China by	2020	11.6
Average growth rate since	2000	6.2
Average growth rate in	1990s	5.6
Average growth rate in	1980s	5.6

Source: Will India Catch-up with China? Mohan Guruswamy et al., Centre for Policy Alternatives, New Delhi.

China is today the world's manufacturing hub. India should emerge as the world's technology and IT (information technology) hub, if it follows pro-active policies. India and China thus have a lot to learn from each other's experience, and can be dynamic partners, rather than competitors in the globalized world.

References

Chang, Gordon G., "The Coming Collapse of China", Random House, New York, 2001.

Gary S. Baker, "Chug Along with China", ET, 2003.

Jayati Ghosh, "Divergent Development Models", *Frontline*, September 9, 2005.

Mohan Guruswamy et al., "Will India Catch-up with China"?, Centre for Policy Alternatives, New Delhi, 2005.

Palley, Thomas I., "The End of Export-led Growth: Implications for Emerging Countries and the Global Economy", Briefing Paper No. 6, Friedrich Ebert Stiftung, Shanghai, March, 1-8, 2011.

Panitchpakdi, Supachai and Mark L. Clifford, "China and the WTO:

Changing China, Changing World Trade", John Wiley and Songs (Asia) Ptd. Ltd.: Singapore, 2002.

Park, J., "Canonical Co-integration Regression", *Econometrica*, 60, 1992, 119-143.

Pedroni, P., "Critical Values for Co-integration Tests in Heterogeneous Panels with Multiple Regressors", *Oxford Bulletin of Economics and Statistics*, Special Issue, 1999, 653-670.

Prasad, Eswar S., "Effects of the Financial Crisis on the US-China Economic Relationship", *Cato Journal*, 29(2), 2009, 223-235.

Qureshi, Mahvash Saeed and Guanghua Wan, "Trade Expansion of China and India: Threat or Opportunity"?, *The World Economy*, 31(10), 2008, 1327-1350.

Ram, R., "Exports and Economic Growth in Developing Countries: Evidence from Time-series and Cross-section Data", *Economic Development and Cultural Change*, 36(1), 1987, 51-72.

Rodrik, Dani and Arvind Subramanian, "From 'Hindu Growth' to Productivity Surge: The Mystery of the Indian Growth Transition", IMF Working Papers 04/77, 2004, International Monetary Fund.

Saighal, Vinod, "Re-structuring South Asian Security", Manas Publications, New Delhi, 2000.

Shroff, Minoo R, "China's Remarkable Economic Growth: Some Lessons", Forum of Free Enterprise, Mumbai, 2000.

Stock, J. and Watson, M., "A Simple Estimator of Co-integrating Vectors in Higher Order Integrated Systems", *Econometrica*, 61, (4), 1993, 783-820.

Tam, S.Y., "Can Malaysian Manufacturing Compete with China in WTO?", *Asia-Pacific Development Journal*, 8(2), 2001.

Tang, Sumei, E., A. Selvanathan and S. Selvanathan, "Foreign Direct Investment, Domestic Investment and Economic Growth in China: A Time Series Analysis", *The World Economy*, 31(10), 2008, 1292-1309.

Thorbeckc, W., "Investigating the Effect of Exchange Rate Changes on Chinese Processed Exports", *Journal of Japanese and International Economics*, 25(2), 2011, 33-46.

Tony Nash, "China or India: It's China and India", *Economic Times*, May 11, 2005.

Wadhva, Charan D., "Geo-economic Positioning of India's Trade and Allied Relations: Perspectives on India's Experience with

Regional Integration" in V.A. Pai Panandiker and Ashis Nandy (eds.), Contemporary India, Tata McGraw Hill Publishing Company Ltd. New Delhi.

Yasheng Huang and Tarun Khanna, "Can India Overtake China?", *Foreign Policy*, July-August, 2003.

9

Indo-Australian Economic Co-operation

Destination India seems to be the latest buzzword in business circles down under. India-Australia bilateral trade stood at AU$ 15.2 billion in 2013, up from AU$ 5.1 billion in 2003. The current economic scenario in India presents opportunities for Australian businesses in sectors such as agriculture, energy, mining and services sector.

Traditionally, Australian companies have focused on Far-eastern nations like China, Indonesia, Japan, Singapore, Thailand and Korea due to logistical advantage and lower tariffs. But now, the Australian giants have realized India's huge market potential.

As an indicator, Australia's trade with China stands at nearly four times that of India. However, India is now being perceived as the "second" China due to its huge market size. Going by the present trends, it is expected that India will equal China in about five year's time.

The sectors that have attracted attention are minerals, specialized telecom and IT hardware, and processed foods, fruits and vegetables. However, emerging areas include environment management products, medical hardware, health consultancy services, hospital management, tourism, film production and specialized IT software.

Infrastructure sector is another area that is seeing participation of Australian companies. Three Australian companies are participating in Sahara Group's flagship project, Amby Valley, in terms of designing and development.

Similarly, several Indian companies are also vying for the Australian market. Birla and Sterlite have recently bought two mines in Australia. Other sectors attracting Indian corporates include IT, minerals, and steel and steel products.

The Australian and Indian Governments are dedicated to improving competitiveness and to building greater links between their economies and regional and global economies. They are also giving a more active role to business. Regulatory burdens that government has in the past placed upon business are being drastically reduced. These reforms will further strengthen their economies and their bilateral commercial ties.

The private sector has responded strongly to the new environment. These reform processes have put Australia and India in a position where they are very competitive in Asia-Pacific markets. India has recognized that economic dynamism can only be achieved by releasing the energies of the private sector, and by integrating with the world economy. India's influence in East Asia and the broader Asia-Pacific region will only grow in the years ahead. The pattern of trade too has shifted, with India's exports to the Asia-Pacific region far outpacing the growth of exports to any other region.

Indo-Australian Bilateral Engagement

In the post-Pokharan-2 and post-September 11 world, Indo-Australian relations have taken on a new meaning. India's "Look East" and "Extended Neighbourhood" policy initiated in the early 1990s, has acquired new dimensions in Australia. Despite past misgivings, India is being recognized "Down Under" as economically, culturally and politically compatible. The shared "British Commonwealth" legacy of parliamentary democratic pluralism, respect for private property and rule-of-the-law, and of course the English language, have brought new economic and strategic complementarities to Indo-Australian relations. Australia's "Look West" policy now goes beyond the ASEAN region to include India in her economic and strategic calculations.

There is growing realisation on both sides to step-up economic cooperation. A perception perhaps lingers in Canberra that India, could become a rival if India is allowed greater access to the Asia-Pacific region; but the emergence of China as a major economic and strategic player in the region, has tempered Australian misconceptions. India's growing diplomatic clout in the ASEAN, her economic dynamism, rapid modernization and integration with the world economy, will only strengthen Indo-Australian relations.

Thus, from a phase of "benign neglect", the two countries have reached the stage of "realisation of the potential". India is now certainly more than a small "blimp" on Australia's economic and strategic radar screen.

Australian and Indian Economies

India has gone through more than a decade of economic reforms. Beginning in 1991, the thrust of reforms was fiscal stabilization, and initiation of major structural reforms aimed at industrial deregulation and globalization to induce accelerated investment, growth and employment.

The financial sector reforms have been brought into balance with sustainable balance of payments, foreign currency assets at US$ 100 billion, and a comfortable servicing of debt-repayments. Inflation levels are at record lows of less than 5 percent in the last five years, and poverty has fallen from 36 percent in the early 1990s to less than 26 percent in 2001-2002. However, there have been major infrastructural bottlenecks—inadequate good-quality roads and lack of serious reforms in the power sector. The information technology (IT) sector has also made rapid strides, and India has emerged as a key player in IT and IT-enabled services.

The key disappointment of the 1990s has been inadequate employment generation—with employment elasticities rapidly coming down in the organized sector. There has also been an "absolute" fall in agricultural employment.

Second generation reforms have already been initiated, and it is hoped that acceleration in economic growth and exports will follow, without significant changes in the socio-political parameters. India is now focusing on labour-market reforms and disinvestment in the public sector, besides speeding up the liberalization and globalization process.

Australia's open free-market economy was further liberalized in 1988, with the federal Governments' financial deregulation of the economy. Trade rationalization in consonance with APEC (Asia Pacific Economic Co-operation) guidelines, competition policies, labour market reforms, and accelerating overall competitiveness, are some of the other features of the Australian economy in the new millennium.

The Australian economy has shifted away from dependence on resources (particularly mining) and agriculture-based industries to a wide range of financial and service-oriented industries. The biggest growth areas are IT-based, where Australia, like India is in some areas, well into the forefront of the new technology age.

Australia's open and efficient regulatory environment, sound legal system for dispute settlement and contract enforcement has placed it well to attract foreign investment. It has an increasingly large pool of professionals working in IT, engineering, legal, accounting, and management consulting, gelling well with the old economy sectors of mining, oil and gas and agri-business.

Australia is no longer reliant upon exports of agricultural and mining products. It is now increasingly a source of high-value added manufactures and services. Trade now amounts to fully 40 percent of Australia's GDP, up from 30 percent only ten years ago. Manufactures now total over 30 percent of merchandise exports. Services amount to nearly a quarter of all exports. These reform processes have put Australia in a position, where it is now very competitive in Asia-Pacific markets.

Australian investment in India covers banking and financial services, manufacturing, telecommunications, hotels, mineral processing, food processing, oil and gas and automotive parts. The largest Australian investment in India is the Bank Standard Chartered/ANZ. Other Australian companies doing business in India are BHP, RTZ-CRA, Telstra and News Corporation and Lumley Technologies.

Indian motor vehicles like the Suzuki Alto and the Maruti Jeep are also making an impression in the Australian markets. Thus, there is vast scope for Indo-Australian bilateral investment facilitation and co-operation.

Indo-Aussie Business Ties

The Australian domestic market remains small to medium by world standards, and in many of the industries, the success and growth factors are from "exports" or "potential exports". Australian tariff barriers have been considerably lowered, and the objective will be to keep on lowering them, so as to make import-substitution competitive and favourable for business development.

Effort has been made by both governments and industry chambers to increase awareness about potential business opportunities. The scenario has changed recently, as India gets access to international money markets for making overseas investment through ADR/GDR issues.

The match between Indian resources and expertise, with those in Australia will often lead to profitable business ventures. Tourism and the hospitality industries have been areas that have witnessed considerable growth, and hold lot of future potential.

Sports, entertainment and their media links are also areas, which can be strengthened in the years to come.

Australia's leading Fosters beer is now bottled in India, and has been proven successful in many cities.

The Indian entertainment industry, particularly Hindi films, has been a major factor in bringing Australia closer to India. After seeing Indian movies many Indians want to visit Australia, with their projection of Australia's scenic beauty, particularly the Sydney Opera House. Over thirty Indian movies have been shot in Australia, and many more are in the pipeline. Australia offers some of the most picturesque shooting spots, and post-production facilities for film shooting.

Summing Up

In conclusion, there is growing realisation by both Australia and India to step-up trade, investments, and dialogue. However, some of the problem areas are:

- Australian companies face problems on account of obstinate lower-level Indian bureaucrats, who often renege on unwritten commitments.
- Multifarious clearances are required at various levels stifling any fresh business ideas.
- Australian companies can help India in exploiting its vast mineral resources to India's advantage, as Australia has superior and time-tested expertise in mineral exploitation.
- Information technology, environment technology, health and tourism are some of the areas where Indo-Aussie collaboration can be intensified.
- Australia also offers excellent and reasonable high-quality higher education compatible with the Indian system. Many Indian students now study in Australian Universities, and the educational flow will only grow in the years to come.
- Inter-State differences in environmental norms of India and the fact that mining is a State subject also hampers greater Australian investment to India.

Thus, sustained bilateral economic engagement and strategic interaction can take Indo-Australian relations to a higher diplomatic plane.

References

Barua, Amit, "Renewing Indo-Australian Ties", *Frontline,* 13th May 2001, 49-50.

"Economic Survey", Government of India, Ministry of Finance.

"India-New Economy, Old Economy", Department of Foreign Affairs and Trade, Commonwealth of Australia, 2001.

Iyer, Nandini, "India and the Indian Ocean", APH Publishing House, New Delhi, 1985.

Janelle, Bonor, "Australia-India Security Relations: Common Interest or Common Disinterest?", Working Paper, No. 67, New South Wales, Australian Defence Studies Centre, April 2001.

Kenneth McPherson, Pai Panandiker and Marika Vicziamy (eds.), "Australia and India in the Context of the Indian Ocean and APEC Regions", Centre for Policy Research, New Delhi, 2000 (Mimeo).

World Bank, *World Development Reports.*

10

India-Singapore Comprehensive Economic Partnership

Introduction

The city state of Singapore is strategically located at a critical intersection of international commerce, and in the geo-strategic vicinity of India and China. Singapore commands attention on the international stage as a dynamic economy, and according to Michael Leifer as an "exceptional state".

India's links with Southeast Asia goes back to centuries. India has left the imprint of its great civilization all over the region—in religion, culture, arts and literature. However, during the first four decades after India's Independence, India turned inwards. Its priority was self-sufficiency rather than interdependence, and these historic linkages weakened. Today, India is once again opening up and rediscovering the region. It is attracting investments from all over the world, especially in IT (information technology). Outward investments from India have also been increasing. Its external trade has increased, and with Southeast Asia, trade has multiplied six times in the last ten years. If the reforms continue, India's interests and influence in the region will continue to grow. India's "Look East" policy and economic liberalization efforts coincided with Singapore's regionalization strategy of investing in emerging economies, providing a common ground for cooperation. Singapore is a natural gateway for India to engage in the region, because of its historical ties and special friendship between the two countries.

There have been many high-level visits exchanged between the two countries, including heads of state and heads of government visits. Bilateral agreements on avoidance of double taxation, cooperation in shipping, tourism, civil aviation, information technology and science and technology have been signed between India and Singapore.

Singapore also played a leading role in India becoming a member of the ARF (ASEAN Regional Forum) and the ASEAN+1 Summit. Among the ASEAN states, Singapore has gone the farthest to improve both bilateral and associational ties. India's former Prime Minister P.V. Narasimha Rao, in his path-breaking Singapore lecture of September 1994, which set in motion India's "Look East" policy said, "The Asia-Pacific could be the spring board for our leap into the global market place. I am happy to have had this opportunity to enunciate my belief in this vision of a new relationship between India and the Asia-Pacific from Singapore, which I consider the geographic and symbolic centre of the Asia-Pacific". Since then, Singapore has been the key country for India's engagement with Southeast Asia. It was the country coordinator for the ASEAN-India dialogue. Singapore's exertions on behalf of India are openly acknowledged by the Indian policy making community.

During his visit to Singapore in August 2003, the then Indian External Affairs Minister candidly noted, "...in the development of our ties with ASEAN, few countries have been as creative and pro-active as Singapore. We are grateful to our many friends here, in particular, (then) Prime Minister Goh Chok Tong, for his vision and leadership in bringing India and ASEAN closer.

This has been made possible by virtue of the strong bilateral relationship that India and Singapore have built over the years". Prime Minister Lee Hsien Loong, in a speech in New Delhi in July 2005, noted, "...India's influence is being felt all over Southeast Asia. In Singapore alone, there are more than 1,500 Indian companies. Many are regional headquarters, some even overseeing operations in the Indian market. Thousands of Indian professionals work in Singapore in IT, financial services and other fields. Bollywood movies enjoy a strong following...the stage has been set for a burgeoning bilateral relationship between Singapore and India, and wider and deeper cooperation between India and Southeast Asia. With greater collaboration and integration between the people of both sides, and continued reforms by those in Government, we can look forward to a vibrant and dynamic future for Asia".

The increasingly close relations between India and Singapore in recent years have been underpinned by a dramatic growth in bilateral trade and investment links. The major items of Indian exports to Singapore are textile manufactures including apparel and yarn, precious stones and pearls, parts for office and data machines, aluminium, electrical machinery, fish and fish products and fruits and vegetables. The major items of India's imports from Singapore have been petroleum products, machinery, metallic ores/scrap, organic chemicals, primary plastics and scientific instruments. Singapore's economy complements India's economy, and does not threaten India's sensitive sectors. Singapore-India trade was US$ 19.3 billion in 2013-14, making Singapore the 7th largest trading partner of India, globally. Singapore can therefore play a useful role as a pathfinder for India.

The CECA (Comprehensive Economic Cooperation Agreement) between India and Singapore created the necessary conducive environment for a strong bilateral relationship, and wider cooperation between India and Southeast Asia. CECA combines liberalized commercial transactions in goods and services, with two-way investment flows in untapped areas. It is a very big psychological step for India, signifying a new direction in India's economic diplomacy. It is India's first overarching economic pact with any country. Integral to the CECA is a wide array of established practices and proposed initiatives, ranging from dispute settlement arrangements and a review mechanism to an updated avoidance of double-taxation and other measures. India through the CECA has moved from the old policy of substantial self sufficiency to one where it wants to link up and open up markets in a controlled sort of way, and encourage linkages and exchanges. The CECA lays the groundwork for agreements with many other countries.

With a cumulative investment of US$ 25.5 billion from April 2000 to March 2014, Singapore has emerged as the second largest foreign investor in the country. The major investments in India from Singapore are channelised through three major agencies: Government of Singapore Investment Corporation, Monetary Authority of Singapore and Temasak Holdings. Many Indian companies, mainly trading and software companies have set up joint ventures and subsidiaries in Singapore to promote their business activities in the region, covering diverse product areas such as automobile ancillaries, precision tooling, palm kernel processing, micro and mini computers.

In the tourism sector, opportunities are emerging rapidly for Singapore as Indian tourists have become the highest spenders among the tourists to Singapore, and the fourth largest revenue generating market, with growing affluence among the Indian middle class. In the logistics sector, the Port of Singapore Authority (PSA) has been involved in port development and management in Tuticorin in Tamil Nadu and Piparav in Gujarat. These developments have the potential to lead to major investment opportunities for other Singapore firms in the logistics sector.

Defence-related research could be an area of future cooperation. Incremental interactions have taken place across a wide spectrum, ranging from education and culture. Singapore is also keen that India plays an appropriate role in a "creative fashion" in the maintenance of security along the Straits of Malacca.

Singapore Economy

A former colonial trading port, serving the regional economies of maritime Southeast Asia, Singapore aspired to be a "global city" serving world markets and major multinational corporations. A quarter century after Independence in 1965, the city-state had become a manufacturing centre with one of the highest incomes in the region. As one of Asia's four "little dragons" or newly industrializing economies, Singapore along with the Republic of Korea (South Korea), Taiwan, and Hong Kong was characterized by an export-oriented economy, relatively equitable income distribution, trade surpluses with the United States and other developed countries, and a common heritage of Chinese civilization and Confucian values. The small island had no resources other than its strategic location and the skills of its nearly 2.7 million people. It has claimed a set of economic superlatives in the 1980s, including the world's busiest port, the world's highest rate of annual economic growth (11 percent), and the world's highest savings rate (42 percent of income).

Singapore has lived by international trade, as it had since its founding in 1819, and operated as a free port with free markets. Its small population and dependence on international markets meant that regional and world markets were larger than domestic markets, which presented both business managers and government policymakers with distinctive economic challenges and opportunities. The value of Singapore's international trade was more than three times its gross domestic product (GDP). The country's year-to-year economic performance fluctuated unpredictably with the cycles of world markets, which were beyond the control or even the influence of Singapore's leaders. In periods of growing international trade, such as the 1970s, Singapore could reap great gains, but even relatively minor downturns in world trade could produce deep recession in the Singapore economy, as happened in 1985-86. The country's dependence on and vulnerability to international markets shaped the economic strategies of Singapore's leaders.

The economy rests on five major sectors: the regional entrepôt trade; export-oriented manufacturing; petroleum refining and shipping; production of goods and services for the domestic economy; and the provision of specialized services for the international market, such as banking and finance, telecommunications, and tourism. The spectacular growth of manufacturing in the 1970s and 1980s had a major impact on the economy and the society, but tended to obscure what carried over from the economic structure of the past. Singapore's economy always depended on international trade and on the sale of services. An entrepôt was essentially a provider of services such as wholesaling, warehousing, sorting and processing, credit, currency exchange, risk management, ship repair and provisioning, business information, and the adjudication of commercial disputes. In this perspective, which focused on exchange and processing, the 1980s assembly of electronic components and manufacture of precision optical instruments were evolutionary steps from the nineteenth century sorting and grading of pepper and rubber. Both processes used the skills of Singaporeans to add value to commodities that were produced elsewhere and destined for consumption outside the city-state.

The dependence on external markets and suppliers pushed Singapore toward economic openness, free trade, and free markets. In the 1980s, Singapore was a free port with only a few revenue tariffs and a small set of protective tariffs scheduled for abolition in the 1990s. It had no foreign exchange controls or domestic price controls. There were no controls on private enterprise or investment, nor any limitations on profit remittance or repatriation of capital.

Foreign corporations were welcome, foreign investment was solicited, and full 70 percent of the investment in manufacturing was foreign. The government provided foreign and domestic enterprises with a high-quality infrastructure, efficient and graft-free administration, and a sympathetic concern for the problems of businesses.

The vulnerability inherent in heavy dependence on outside markets impelled Singapore's leaders to buffer their country's response to perturbations in world markets and to take advantage of their country's ability to respond to changing economic conditions. Unable to control so much that affected their nation's prosperity, they concentrated on those domestic institutions that could be controlled. The consequence was an economy characterized by a seemingly paradoxical adherence to free trade and free markets in combination with a dominant government role in macroeconomic management and government control of major factors of production such as land, labour, and capital. The extraordinarily high domestic savings rate provided reserves to weather such economic storms as trade recessions and generated a pool of domestically controlled capital that could be invested to serve the long-term interests of Singapore rather than of foreign corporations.

The high savings rate, however, was the result of carefully formulated government programs, which included a compulsory contribution of up to 25 percent of all salaries to a government-controlled pension fund. The government held about 75 percent of the country's land, was the largest single employer, controlled the level of wages, and housed about 88 percent of the population in largely self-owned apartments. It also operated a set of wholly-owned government enterprises and held stock in additional domestic and foreign firms. Government leaders, deeply aware of Singapore's need to sell its services in a competitive international market, continually stressed the necessity for the citizens to master high levels of skills and to subordinate their personal wishes to the good of the community. The combination of devotion to free-market principles and the need for internal control and discipline in order to adapt to the demands of markets reminded observers of many family firms, and residents of the country commonly referred to it as Singapore Inc.

With a limited domestic market and almost no natural resources, Singapore was forced to integrate into the global economy early in its development. When Singapore separated from Malaysia, it lost its hinterland. It had no choice but to swiftly shift to an export-driven industrialization policy, slashing trade barriers and actively seeking foreign investment. This change in orientation brought Singapore an average growth rate of 10 percent from 1965 to 1979. In 1965, when Singapore first became independent, its total trade amounted to S$ 6.8 billion. As in 2013, exports from Singapore amounted to US$ 410.3 billion and imports constituted US$ 373 billion. The country's GDP in terms of PPP for the above period stood at US$ 348.7 billion. The continued rapid economic development over the past years owes much to its open trade regime, clearly directed economic management and its position in the centre of a dynamic regional market. Political stability and a well developed infrastructure combined with very high rates of savings and investment, and attractive investment incentives have contributed to making the economy one of the strongest in the world.

Singapore is a highly industrialized economy. Agriculture and mining are of little importance. Their contribution to GDP is close to zero. 90 percent of food consumed in Singapore is imported. Financial and business services and manufacturing are the most important sectors accounting for 27 percent and 28 percent of GDP respectively. The most important manufacturing sector is electronics directly accounting for 52.5 percent of manufacturing export.

By tapping into the global grid of trade, investments, and capital, Singapore recorded an average annual growth rate of 7.3 percent and the nominal value of its non-oil domestic exports have grown by an average of 12 percent per annum. Singapore's trade to GDP ratio is the highest in the world. The importance of trade to Singapore is illustrated by the fact that since 1999, Singapore's total trade in goods and services has accounted on average for nearly 360 percent of GDP. Singapore is thus an advocate of the multilateral trading system as free trade has been crucial for its survival.

Singapore's sound macroeconomic policies, coupled with its openness helped it to recover rapidly from the effects of the Asian financial crisis. The Singapore economy recovered in 1999 and 2000 to register GDP growth of 6.9 percent and 9.7 percent respectively. This growth was fuelled by growth in IT spending as a result of the dot.com boom.

Trade Performance and Policy Options

Singapore's external trade pattern reflects the conditions in the external environment. Its major trading partners in trade in commercial services are China, Malaysia, US, EU, Japan, and the regional developing economies. The top ten trading partners account for more than three-fourths of Singapore's trade in services. The geographical pattern of Singapore's trade in services is thus broadly similar to trade in goods.

Singapore's trade policy directions are underpinned by several factors:

- Constraints of a small domestic market with limited natural resources.
- Its dependence on the global economy; Singapore's economy is plugged into the international grid and cannot be insulated from key global trends. It is vulnerable to developments around the world.
- Its dependence on free access to markets around the world for its economic survival and growth.

The stated objectives of Singapore's trade policies are: to contribute towards the strengthening of a free, open and stable multilateral trading system; to develop Singapore into an international trading centre; to identify new markets while maintaining existing markets; to safeguard and diversify sources of imports; and to increase services exports. In general, Singapore maintains one of the most liberal trading regimes in the world. It has very few trade barriers and provides a favourable climate for trade cooperation for countries both in the immediate vicinity and beyond. It primarily follows a free trade policy.

Singapore's prosperity is thus inextricably linked to that of the region and the world. To secure and expand its political and economic space, Singapore has adopted a multi-pronged approach in pursuing trade liberalization initiatives through the multilateral trading system, bilateral free trade agreements

(FTAs), regional trading arrangements (RTAs), and through regional groupings such as ASEAN, APEC, and ASEM (Asia-Europe Meeting).

Singapore needs to ensure that it remains integrated with the rest of the world through deeper multilateral, regional, and bilateral links. In light of these challenges, Singapore's policy is to continue to promote greater integration at the multilateral, regional, and bilateral levels. It will continue to adopt a multi-pronged approach to trade policy by engaging in bilateral and regional FTA negotiations. It will continue to play a proactive role at the WTO to keep the momentum of multilateral trade liberalization.

Investment Climate and Policies

Singapore is located at the heart of Southeast Asia which is a resource rich region with a market potential of some 300 million people. Thus, Singapore is well placed to serve the fast growing markets of this region. Singapore's unique location and sophisticated telecommunications network allow financial institutions and other companies in the country to transact business with any part of the world within the same working day. Singapore has first-class infrastructure in telecommunications and transport particularly in sea and air. Singapore's Changi Airport has the most air links in the Asia-Pacific.

Singapore has seven free trade zones (FTZs), six for sea-borne cargo and one for air cargo within which a wide range of facilities and services are provided for storage and re export of dutiable and controlled goods. Goods can be stored within the zones without any customs documentation until they are released in the market. They can also be processed and re-exported with minimum customs formalities. The FTZs at the port facilitate entrepot trade and promote the handling of transhipment cargo. They offer free 72-hour storage for import/re-export of cargo.

The Economic Development Board (EDB) promotes foreign investments with a borderless view beyond Singapore and into the region. As Singapore's investment architect, it helps foreign as well as local companies plan global business strategies and configure their activities from their base in Singapore. The EDB adds value to investors by providing a one-stop investment promotion service to identify business opportunities in Singapore and the region, and helps them set up their operations speedily.

Singapore's regulatory environment is business-friendly and is characterized by transparency and clarity. The bureaucracy is generally considered to be efficient and effective. Prior to implementing any law or regulation, the government usually consults relevant bodies and agencies, companies and the public. Various rules and regulations relating to tax, labour, banking, finance, industrial health and safety, arbitration, wages and training are formulated and reviewed with the interests of foreign investors and local enterprises in mind. However, local laws give regulatory bodies, wide discretion to modify and impose new conditions. This allows government agencies to negotiate the way they provide incentives or other services to foreign companies on a case-by-case basis.

Singapore has a highly open investment regime, through which it seeks to overcome land and labour constraints. It aims to progress into the league of developed countries by attracting firms that can build up the country's technological base and labour force capabilities. Moreover, attracting foreign investment into the country has been an economic strategy of the government since Independence. Consequently, the country's legal framework and public policies have always been investor-friendly.

The government of Singapore generally does not restrict or discourage foreign investment either to protect local industries or for any other reasons. However, restrictions on investment in a limited number of sectors exist. Armament manufacturing is strictly closed to foreign investment. Other sectors where foreign investments are limited include news media, telecommunications, broadcasting and domestic banking. Moreover; there can be no foreign ownership of public utility services. Incentives are used both for the promotion of new investments in industries and services and for encouraging existing companies to upgrade through mechanization and automation and through the introduction of new products and services.

India-Singapore Trade

Singapore is the largest market in ASEAN for India's merchandise exports, followed by Malaysia, Thailand, Indonesia, and the Philippines.

Singapore is India's largest trading and investment partners in ASEAN. The increasingly close relations between India and Singapore in recent years have been underpinned by a dramatic growth in bilateral trade and investment linkages. India is looking for infrastructure investments, critical technologies and export markets. Singapore has surplus capital and could be a useful partner in infrastructure development in India as well as investment in Indian companies.

Major Items of India's Exports: The major items of India's exports to Singapore include crude petroleum, refined motor spirit, petroleum oils, polished diamonds for jewellery, polished industrial diamonds, articles of jewellery, aluminium unwrought, aluminium sheets, parts and accessories of computers, synthetic fabrics, silk fabrics, embroidery, table linen of man-made fibres, combed cotton, knitted T-shirts, vests, benzene, dyes, acids, insecticides, fungicides, household articles of stainless steel, corrugated products of iron and steel, forged/stamped articles of iron and steel, bars and rods of iron steel, parts of boring or sinking machinery, x-ray tubes, medical surgical dental or veterinary instruments/appliances, penicillin, rice, sugar, cashew nuts, essential oil, crabs live/dried, fish (fresh/chilled/dried), titanium ore, menthol, diesel/semi-diesel generating sets, static converters, valves/taps cocks for pipes, boilers, tanks etc, bus/lorry tyres, tobacco. These items in value terms constitute over 70 percent of India's exports to Singapore.

Major Items of India's Imports: The major items of India's imports from Singapore include accessories of computers and computer peripherals, integrated circuits, cellular phones, CD ROMs, styrene, p-xylene, o-Xylene, polypropylene, vinyl acetate, topped crudes, and parts of boring and sinking machinery. Nickel, tin (unwrought), lead (unwrought) aluminium (unwrought), zinc (unwrought), waste and scrap of iron and steel, photographic chemicals, sewing machines, ball/roller bearings, parts for bulldozers, parts of aeroplanes/helicopters, parts for audio/video recorders, medical instruments and appliances, parts of cellular phones, parts of motor vehicles, cigarettes, pigments, parts of cathode ray tubes, auto parts, parts for electrical machines and apparatus. These items in value terms constitute over 60 percent of India's imports from Singapore.

The Singapore Business Federation (SBF), which is the government-guided amalgamation of different chambers of commerce and industry, is also likely to open an office in India. Individual chambers of commerce associated with SBF such as the Chinese, Malay and Indian chambers might also open their own separate offices.

While Singapore's manufacturing base centring on electronics and petrochemicals, and its role as an entrepot centre will continue to sustain the merchandise trade, the emerging opportunities are largely in the services sector, particularly in the information and communication technology (ICT), logistics services, business and financial services, tourism, and health services. This is more so as Singapore plans to develop itself into a service hub and improve its capabilities in areas where there exist considerable complementarities with India. The opportunities are not only in trade in services transactions (such as used by Singapore Airlines of India as a base for some of its IT-enabled services) but also in investments (presence of Indian ICT, pharmaceutical, and trading companies in Singapore, and Singapore's investments in India's ICT, tourism and health services, besides in port development and logistics). The probable involvement of Singapore's polytechnics in technical education in Tamil Nadu, and perhaps other states, could further strengthen bilateral linkages.

The Infocomm Development Authority of Singapore (IDA) has signed an MoU with India's premier IT training company, National Institute of Information Technology (NIIT) to persuade IT professionals to locate in Singapore, from anywhere in the world. As Indian professionals are internationally competitive and culturally compatible, India is among the largest sources of IT manpower in the world and a significant proportion is likely to be sourced from India. This could create a dynamic Indian Diaspora with positive externalities for both the countries. The investments by Singapore Telecom (SingTel) in India's telecom sector in partnership with India's Bharti Televentures to take advantage of India's huge potential domestic telecom and internet market is also another example in this sector.

In the tourism sector, opportunities are emerging rapidly for Singapore as Indian tourists have become the highest spenders among tourists to Singapore and became the fourth largest revenue generating market, with growing affluence among the Indian middle class. Singapore tourism authorities has also been actively involved in promoting select areas in India as a tourism destination for Singaporeans, through a joint marketing by the Government of India tourism office already established in Singapore.

Indeed, Singapore's two airlines, Singapore Airlines and Silk Air have quite liberal rights to fly to several destinations in India. They could however take greater advantage of India's open sky policies concerning air cargo. In the logistics sector, the Port of Singapore Authority (PSA) has been involved in port development and management in Tuticorin in Tamil Nadu and Piparav in Gujarat. These have the potential to lead to major investment opportunities for other Singapore firms in the logistics sector.

Negotiations between Singapore's largest supermarket operator, NTUC Fairprice which has close links with the government, and India's Apollo Group, one of Asia's largest hospital and healthcare management companies to set up a pharmacy and retail chain of convenience stores numbering in the hundreds in petrol stations run by the Indian Oil Corporation also hold promise for greater economic linkages. It would contribute to Singapore's food security, and to its supply chain for other essential household goods. Indian IT companies have recognized the importance of Singapore as a marketing and development centre, and their presence is growing. As Indian businesses have been given much greater freedom to invest abroad, presence of Indian companies from other sectors in Singapore is also increasing. This should also have a positive impact on Singapore's importance as a business hub, and on trade in business services.

Singapore intends to increasingly rely at the margin on investment income from abroad. Its rather large forex reserves of US$ 273.25 billion (August 2014), are mostly invested abroad through holding companies of the Singapore government. It is suggested that these holding companies consider passive investments in infrastructure projects in India. Setting up of a physical presence in India by the Singapore Government Investment Corporation (SGIC), and other such Singapore government investment companies, merits serious consideration. Currently, these holding companies do act in a limited way as venture capitalists for Indian IT companies. However, there is much greater scope in not only the IT sector but also in biotechnology, life sciences, and other areas. For these purposes also, physical presence in India would be beneficial.

Comprehensive Economic Co-operation Agreement (CECA)

On June 29, 2005, India and Singapore signed a Comprehensive Economic Co-operation Agreement (CECA), the first of its kind for India, concluding two years of intensive negotiations. Its distinctive feature is that it is indeed 'comprehensive' and covers trade in goods and services, investment flows and encompasses a double taxation avoidance agreement (DTAA). Such wide-ranging agreements are, in a sense, the logical next step in a world economy increasingly driven by the flows of trade in goods, services and movement of capital.

For India, it seems the gains driving the partnership with Singapore would be in the area of services exports and in-bound FDI. Singapore accounted for approximately 2.5 percent of India's FDI inflows from 1991 to 2005 and has been investing especially in Indian infrastructure industries such as ports, telecommunications and banks, in the last few years. The Singapore government has in the past indicated its willingness to set up a US$ 1 billion fund to invest in India after the CECA comes into force. Since the island-nation is a free-trading port, most of the duties on its tariff lines are zero and there is much it can offer by way of tariff concessions, though the hope is that synergies in Indian manufacturing and Singaporean branding expertise can be tapped to profit in the ASEAN market. One of the difficult aspects of the negotiations was determining the rules of origin (ROO) by which the nationality of goods are determined to ensure that only citizens of the contracting country avail of trade concessions, as there were concerns in India that exporters from third countries could use the Singapore route to dump cheap goods in the country.

The Prime Minister of Singapore, Lee Hsien Loong, believes that the main advantage for Singapore from the agreement is tariff less access to the Indian market in a large number of goods. Besides, some banks will have access to the Indian market. For the Indian side, the big gain from the agreement is on the movement of professionals. Also, inward investment into India from Singapore has become very attractive.

The CECA with Singapore is a free trade agreement (FTA) and covers trade in goods as also services. Besides investment flows and mutual recognition clauses, it is expected to help Singapore widen its frontiers of international commerce. Singapore has close economic linkages with the U.S., Japan and China among others. The business communities in both countries could now "leverage" on this win-win development.

In the services sector, Indian companies stand to benefit through increased market access in distribution services, including retail trading, business services, market research, legal, environmental management, management consultancy, tourism, real estate, consultancy and advertising, engineering, architecture and computer-related services.

The provisions of the CECA are broad, aiming not only to liberalise bilateral trade in goods and services but also to increase investment and ease visa regulations. The CECA is likely to further enhance Singapore's position as Asia's trade hub, boost Indian trade with East Asia, and encourage more foreign investment in India.

Under the provisions of the CECA, Singapore will cut all duties on goods made in India (excepting tobacco and automobiles), while India will remove or reduce duties on a range of Singaporean products, covering around four-fifths of its exports.

As a first step, India will scrap duties on 506 items immediately and will phase out tariffs on a further 2,202 items over the next four years, also reducing duties on another 2,407 items by 2009. However, it will maintain the current level of duties on a list of 6,551 items from Singapore. The deal also included agreements on trade in services and a commitment to liberalise visa requirements for professionals in 127 fields.

The CECA also opens up India's financial services sector to Singaporean investment, allowing three banks from the city-state viz. DBS Holdings, Overseas-Chinese Banking Corp. and United Overseas Banking, to set up branch operations in India. The three may either set up wholly owned subsidiaries (in which case they will be subject to local regulations) or set up regional branches, in which case they will be limited to opening.

Key Provisions of CECA

Improved Avoidance of Double Taxation Agreement: An Avoidance of Double Taxation Agreement (DTA) provides for avoidance of double taxation of income earned in one contracting state by a resident of the other and makes clear the taxing rights between the two contracting states on all forms of income from cross-border economic activities between the two contracting states. The DTA thus helps to facilitate the flow of trade, investment, technical know-how and expertise between the two contracting states by eliminating double taxation of income.

Singapore and India have agreed on a protocol to improve the existing DTA, which was signed in January 1994. The main improvement to the DTA is that tax residents will enjoy capital gains tax exemption on investments in India. However, a tax resident will not be entitled to the capital gains exemption if its affairs are arranged primarily to take advantage of the benefits of the DTA. In addition, a shell/conduit company with negligible or nil business operations or with no real and continuous business activities in Singapore is disallowed from enjoying the capital gains exemption.

For the purposes of the capital gains tax exemption, a company is not a shell company if:

- It is listed on recognised stock exchanges of the contracting state.
- Its total annual expenditure on operations in the residence state is equal to or more than S$ 200,000 or Indian ₹ 50,00,000 in the respective contracting state as the case may be, in the immediately preceding period of 24 months from the date the gains arise.

The capital gains tax exemption regime of a country is an important consideration for investors and this exemption, which was previously only available to Mauritius, will help promote greater investment flows between Singapore and India.

Trade in Goods: The Trade in Goods chapter provides for tariff concessions that will make Singapore goods more competitive vis-à-vis other foreign imports into India. Tariffs on approximately 75 percent of Singapore's domestic exports will be eliminated or substantially reduced within 5 years. The sectors benefiting would include electrical and electronics, instrumentation, pharmaceuticals, and plastics.

For Singaporean goods entering India, those that qualify for tariff concessions are classified into one of the following categories: immediate elimination, phased elimination and phased reduction. Goods in the immediate elimination category will have tariffs on them eliminated completely when CECA comes into effect. For goods in the phased elimination and phased reduction categories, the reduction to the final tariffs will be phased in over 5 years and the percentage reduction is expressed as a margin of preference over the most favoured nation (MFN) applied rates.

Rules of Origin: Rules of Origin (ROO) identify the "nationality" of a good. They ensure that only Singaporean or Indian goods enjoy the tariff concessions under CECA.

The general rule of origin is a combination of 40 percent local content and a change in tariff classification at the 4-digit level. CECA also take into consideration the unique production pattern of Singapore and provides for a list of products that are exempt from the general rule. For each of these products, a specific rule of origin (e.g., change in tariff classification only) has been crafted.

Customs: Good customs procedures are necessary to ensure the free movement of goods traded between both countries. The lack of such procedures can increase compliance costs and diminish the benefits that result from tariff reduction.

Under CECA, the customs authorities from India and Singapore will:

- Provide an advance ruling on the eligibility of originating goods for preferential tariffs and tariff classification, upon the request of the trader. This will provide traders with greater certainty on the status of their goods at the country of import.
- Enhance the application of risk management to focus on

high-risk goods and facilitate the clearance of low risk consignments. Both authorities will also enhance transparency in regulations so that traders would be fully aware of the requirements and procedures in the respective countries.

Standards and Technical Regulations, Sanitary and Phytosanitary Measures: CECA provides a framework for concluding mutual recognition agreements (MRAs) to eliminate duplicative testing and certification of products to facilitate entry of goods for sale in the respective markets. These sectoral MRAs serve to reduce costs and shorten time to market especially useful for products with short life cycle.

Two sectoral annexes for trade in electrical and electronic products, and telecommunication equipment were concluded under the framework chapter. For products in these two sectors, testing and certification to Indian standards and technical regulations can be done at source. They do not have to be further tested or re-certified on arrival in the market.

The potential benefits are reduction in cost due to elimination of duplicative testing and reduction in time to market for these products to enter the Indian or Singapore market. As most of these products have relatively short life cycles, the result is a reduction in relative cost and improved time to market competitiveness of Singapore certified products entering the Indian market and vice versa. India is expected to make the necessary amendments to its legislation to implement these MRA arrangements. This may take another 12-18 months. Singapore will also be providing technical training for Indian standards bodies so as to enable them to implement the MRA.

Of immediate benefit is the food sectoral annex where Singapore has facilitated the import of egg products, dairy products and packaged drinking water from India. This will widen the sources of supply for these food products in Singapore.

Investment: The investment chapter aims to promote and

protect investments from both countries. Market access for investments is based on the Principle of National Treatment subject to the commitments or reservations undertaken. The chapter contains a number of useful features to protect investments. The key features are highlighted as follows:

- **Beneficiaries:** Citizens and enterprises based in Singapore or India. Indian investors are not required to seek foreign investment approval for coverage under the investment chapter.
- **Broad Range of Investment Instruments:** The chapter covers a broad range of investment instruments and assets, such as equity and debt instruments, intellectual property rights (IPRs) and, business licenses and permits. Investments in the nature of both foreign direct investment (FDI) and portfolio investments are covered.
- **National Treatment:** The chapter accords National Treatment to investors from both countries. The market access feature of this provision is subject to the commitments and reservations undertaken.
- **Expropriation and Compensation:** Both countries cannot expropriate investments, directly or indirectly, without proper legal safeguards. Expropriation must be premised on public purpose and compensation based on market value. Land expropriation will be governed by the domestic legislation of each country.
- **Investor to State dispute settlement:** To give investors greater confidence in investing in either country, both countries have committed to allowing investors, once the investment is established, to take a dispute relating to an obligation under the chapter to an international arbitration tribunal.
- **Free Transfers:** Both countries will allow the investors to freely transfer funds related to their investments, such as capital, profits, dividends and royalties.
- **Joint-Ventures:** India has agreed to bind its recent liberalization measures regulating the ability of current

joint ventures to enter into new joint ventures (India's Press Note 1 of 2005).

- **Real Estate:** India has agreed to bind its new regulations governing investments in the real estate sector (India's Press Note 2 of 2005).
- **Others:** The Indian government has formally recognised Temasek and GIC as distinct entities. They are allowed to each own up to 10 percent of a listed Indian company, similar to other foreign institutional investors (FIIs), as stipulated under current Securities and Exchange Board of India (SEBI) regulations.

Trade in Services: The services chapter ensures that service suppliers in India and Singapore are guaranteed access into each others markets. The key features are highlighted as follows:

- **Market Access:** Both countries may not restrict access into their services market by imposing quantitative restrictions (e.g. numerical quotas on services suppliers that are allowed in the market).
- **National Treatment:** Services suppliers will be granted the same treatment as local service suppliers, i.e., no discrimination.
- **Domestic Regulation:** The chapter ensures that domestic regulations governing the provision of services are reasonable, impartial and objective.
- **Mutual Recognition Agreements (MRAs):** The chapter facilitates the freer movement of people. Professional bodies in the accounting and auditing, architecture, medical (doctors), dental and nursing services sectors in both countries will negotiate agreements, within a year of the signing of CECA, recognising each other's education and professional qualifications. This means that upon the completion of these mutual recognition agreements, Indian and Singaporean professionals from these five professions could be able to practice in Singapore and India respectively. Professional bodies for services sectors not

listed above would also be encouraged to enter into negotiations for MRAs.

Generally, the benefits of the CECA will extend to the citizens, permanent residents, local companies as well as foreign MNCs that are constituted or otherwise organised in India or Singapore. Companies wishing to supply audio-visual, educational, financial and telecommunication services, through commercial presence in India or Singapore, would have to meet ownership or control criteria in order to benefit from the CECA.

Both countries have committed to liberalise various services sectors beyond its WTO commitments.

The sectors which Singapore gets preferential access include business services, construction and related engineering services, financial services, telecommunication services, tourism and travel related services and transport services.

India would be able to enjoy preferential treatment for sectors such as business services, distribution services, education services, environmental services and transportation services.

- For financial services, Singapore owned or controlled financial institutions have been given greater privileges to access the Indian market. In banking, DBS, UOB and OCBC can each set up a wholly owned subsidiary (WOS) in India to enjoy treatment on par with Indian banks in branching, places of operations and prudential requirements. Alternatively, should they choose to set up as branches, they have been allocated a separate quota of 15 branches (for all 3 banks) over 4 years, over and above the quota for all foreign banks.
- For asset management, Singapore owned or controlled fund managers have the additional privilege of offering Indian investors mutual funds and collective investment schemes (CIS) listed on the Singapore Exchange (SGX) as well as exchange traded funds (ETFs). These instruments offered by our asset managers are free from the restriction that they must only invest in entities which have a stake in

Indian companies. India has similarly lifted this limitation for India owned or controlled fund managers. Both Singapore and India owned or controlled fund managers can also invest an additional US$ 250 million in equities and instruments listed on the SGX, including mutual funds, CIS and ETFs. This is in addition to the US$ 1 billion cap that all asset managers can invest abroad.

- Indian banks and financial institutions can take advantage of CECA to expand their activities in Singapore. To this end, Indian banks, that satisfy Singapore's admission criteria, will be given wholesale bank licences and up to 3 bank licences with qualifying full banks privileges. In addition, Indian insurers and capital market intermediaries that satisfy our admission criteria will have open access to set up shop in Singapore.
- For telecommunication services, India will bind its foreign equity limit from 25 percent to 49 percent for most services including basic, cellular and long-distance services and 74 percent for internet and infrastructure services. India will also ensure that telecommunication providers from Singapore are treated fairly, transparently, and are allowed to obtain access to the necessary public infrastructure in order to offer their services, thereby creating a more level playing field in India for the Singapore's telecom providers. On its part, Singapore has made binding commitments for telecommunication services such as basic telecommunication services (facilities-based), mobile services, and value-added network (VAN) services.

Air Services: India and Singapore have reaffirmed their rights and obligations under previous agreements and recognise the importance of air connectivity to support the expansion of tourism, trade and investments. Both countries will review and enhance further air services linkages through the bilateral Air Services Agreement, in future.

Movement of Natural Persons: The cross-border movement of natural persons plays a central role in initiating and supporting trade and investments in goods and services. This chapter enhances trade and investment flows by facilitating easier temporary entry for 4 categories of business persons from India and Singapore:

- Business visitors who are holders of five year multiple journey visa will be permitted to enter and engage in business activities for a period of up to 2 months, which upon request, may be further extended by up to 1 month.
- Short-term service suppliers will be granted temporary entry to service their contracts for an initial period of up to 90 days in the first instance.
- Professionals employed in 127 specific occupations will be allowed entry and stay for up to 1 year or the duration of contract, whichever is less.
- Intra-corporate transferees (i.e. managers, executives and specialists within organisations) will be permitted to stay and work in India and Singapore for an initial period of up to 2 years or the period of the contract, whichever is less. The period of stay may be extended for period of up to 3 years at a time for a total term not exceeding 8 years.

The Movement of Natural Persons chapter does not apply to measures regarding citizenship, residence or employment on a permanent basis. It also does not apply to immigration measures as long as these immigration measures do not nullify or impair the commitments made by either country.

The chapter will grant Singaporean and Indian Citizens and permanent residents, guaranteed entry and stay in each other's country as business visitors, short-term service suppliers, professionals and intra-corporate transferees.

Singapore companies will have certainty when they choose to deploy Singapore staff to help manage their Indian operations. Skilled and qualified professionals and service suppliers from Singapore would also gain easier access to the vast Indian market. Similarly, this would also apply to Indian companies when they deploy Indian staff to manage their operations in Singapore.

With freer movement of business persons between countries, bilateral trade and investment flows should be significantly enhanced. Hence, companies from both countries can leverage on the chapter to drive greater economic integration between India and Singapore.

E-Commerce: Both India and Singapore reaffirm their commitment to promote a liberalised environment for electronic commerce. The chapter on electronic commerce addresses fair treatment of digital products, such as software, e-books and e-movies, coming from Singapore.

The Agreement also prohibits any imposition of customs duties on digital products delivered electronically. In addition, both sides commit to ensuring transparency by making publicly available all relevant laws and regulations affecting electronic commerce.

Intellectual Property: The chapter on Intellectual Property (IP) Cooperation is focused on collaboration and cooperation between the parties.

The parties agreed to undertake and promote mutually beneficial cooperation in the fields of IP and plant variety rights. These forms of cooperation could include the joint organisation of training programs, and collaboration on projects to promote the effective use and application of IP. The parties have specifically identified their leading training centres: the IP Academy, Singapore, and the Intellectual Property Training Institute, Nagpur, as initial partners for cooperation.

The provisions on cooperation and collaboration in IP and training arrived at under the chapter paves the way forward for collaboration between the parties in the development of key IP programmes and IP infrastructure. Singapore and India benefit mutually in terms of potential exchange on IP and IP-related training and education programmes. In addition, the mutual recognition of the importance of plant variety rights means that both Singapore and India will be able to consider cooperation activities in this field.

Science and Technology: The Science and Technology Cooperation chapter will allow for the fostering of closer collaboration in research and development and commercialisation of technologies between the scientific and research communities from the two countries. It expands an earlier agreement on science and technology signed in 1995.

The Agreement is geared towards harnessing the complementary capabilities available in the two countries. The areas of focus that have been identified for possible cooperation are marine and agricultural biotechnology, space research, advance materials and information technology.

Education: The education cooperation chapter is aimed at combining the strengths of the education system in India and Singapore to the mutual benefit of the two countries.

One of its key mandates is to facilitate joint post-graduate programs between the world-renowned Indian Institutes of Technology (IITs) and Institute of Science (IISc) with the Singapore universities. These programs will focus on research and education with clear industrial linkages to companies from both countries. Arising from this, NUS and IIT, Bombay signed an MoU to establish a joint graduate engineering programme. The NUS-IIT-B tie-up was the first alliance by any IIT with a foreign university in a significant manner. The programme will draw heavily on existing NUS and IIT-B infrastructure and course modules. Both IIT-B and NUS professors will participate in joint teaching and supervision of projects. The partnership is expected to yield some 40 MS and eight Ph.D. graduates annually.

The chapter also provides that degrees specified by the University Grants Commission (UGC) of India or an institution of national importance of India, and by universities in Singapore, shall be recognised for the purposes of admission into the universities of both countries. This is in addition to all other admission criteria that must still be satisfied.

A Joint Committee on Education will be established to emphasise the key role that education will play in fostering the relationship between the two countries. Its members will be drawn not only from government but from the private sector as well.

Media: The Media Cooperation chapter offers a platform for the regulatory agencies from both sides to work closely together. This will allow focus not only on regulatory issues of mutual concern, but more importantly on promoting greater industry and private sector collaboration. Some of the areas of collaboration that could be looked into are digital media and convergent services, intellectual property rights, education and training, co-production of film and television content, distribution and marketing, and research and development.

Dispute Settlement: In any international agreement, whilst we do not expect nor hope for disputes between the parties as to what the agreement means, it would nevertheless be prudent to prepare for such an eventuality. In this connection, Singapore and India have negotiated a comprehensive set of dispute settlement procedures. Disputes are subject to consultations, negotiations, conciliation and arbitration just like in the WTO, thereby enhancing the rule of law in international trade.

Review: The ministers of India and Singapore, who are responsible for trade negotiations, will meet within a year of the date of entry into force of CECA for a review. Subsequent reviews will be done biennially or otherwise as appropriate.

Conclusions

The intermeshing of Indian and Singaporean areas of concern in trade augurs well for both countries. Singapore is looking out for viable and lucrative destinations besides China and the U.S., and India is well placed both economically and diplomatically to forge an effective and mutually beneficial partnership. Thus, the increasing diplomatic complementarities and synergies of the two countries in trade and investment, will act as a stabilizing force in the Asia-Pacific region.

References

Bharat Jhunjhunwala, "Singapore FTA: Against Asian Unity?",

Business Line, New Delhi, 2005.

Frederic Gare and Mattoo, A., "India and ASEAN: The Politics of India's Look East Policy", Manohar Publishers, New Delhi, 2001.

Gaur, S., "ASEAN-India Ties Entering a New Phase", *Business Times*, Singapore, 2004.

Goh Chok Tong, "Anchored in Singapore, Connected to the World", Speech at the International Enterprise Forum, Singapore, February 2005.

Jha, P.K, "Reassessing India's Look East Policy", *World Focus*, 287-288, 2003.

Lee Hsien Loong, Speech delivered at the CII, FICCI, ASSOCHAM, Joint Forum, New Delhi, 2005.

Margaret Liang, "Singapore's Trade Policies: Priorities and Options", *ASEAN Economic Bulletin*, Vol. 22, No. 1, 2005.

Rahul Sen, M.G. Asher, and R.S. Rajan, "ASEAN-India Economic Relations: Current Status and Future Prospects", *Economic and Political Weekly*, 2004.

Rajesh Mehta, "Economic Cooperation between India and Singapore: A Feasibility Study", RIS-DP # 41/2003.

Sarma, A. and P.K. Mehta, "Exploring Indo-ASEAN Economic Partnership in a Globalising World", Bookwell, New Delhi, 2002.

Saywell, T., "Singapore's New India Play", *Far Eastern Economic Review*, Singapore, 2001.

Trade Policy Review: Singapore, WTO, Geneva, 2004.

11

India's Regional Trade Agreements (RTAs)

Prior to economic reforms process initiated in 1991, India had adopted a very cautious and guarded approach to regionalism. Recognising that RTAs would continue to feature prominently in world trade, India engaged with its trading partners/blocks with the intention of expanding its export market and began concluding in principle agreements and moving in some cases even towards comprehensive economic cooperation agreements (CECAs) which covers free trade agreement (FTA) in goods, services, investments and identified areas of economic cooperation.

RTAs are an integral part of India's foreign trade policy, complementing the multilateral trading system. Framework agreements have already been entered into with a number of trading partners with specific road maps to be followed and specified timeframes by which the negotiations are to be completed. Joint study groups have also been set up for examining feasibility of CECA between India-Japan, India-Brazil-South Africa and India-Russia. India and European Commission have also set up a high level trade group (HLTG) as mandated by the India-EU Summit held in New Delhi on September 7, 2005. The mandate of the HLTG is to explore ways and means to increase bilateral economic flows including the possible launching of negotiations on a comprehensive trade and investment agreement.

Look East Policy

East Asia—including Japan, China, South Korea and ASEAN—is India's largest trading partner, ahead of EU and the US. India unveiled the *Look East* policy in 1991.

Proliferation of free trade agreements (FTAs) is the clearest evidence of Asian countries' desire to forge closer economic relationships. The growing importance of CECA's indicates that such agreements are becoming deeper, extending to areas beyond just tariff reduction.

Intra-regional trade and investment require building up of shared infrastructure. Many Asian countries have joined together to develop cross-border infrastructure to lay the foundations for closer trading relationships and increased connectivity among countries. The Greater Mekong Sub-region is quite advanced in this endeavour. Similar initiatives are underway in South Asia and in Central Asia, with exciting prospects for future development. The spirit of enhanced monetary cooperation in Asia is evident from initiatives like the Chiang Mai Initiative and the Asian Bond Fund having major potential for financing regional investments.

Asia remains one of the least integrated regions lacking a continent-wide regional organization. Forging closer links among Asian nations through appropriate institutional mechanisms can lead to substantial enhancement of national, regional and global productivity and output. In the past, India had adopted a very cautious approach to regionalism, and was engaged in only a few bilateral/regional initiatives, mainly through preferential trade agreements (PTAs).

Recognising that RTAs would continue to feature in world trade for a long time, and with the intention of expanding its export market, India began concluding in principle agreements as a possible step towards CECAs, which cover FTA in goods (zero customs duty regime within a fixed time frame on items covering substantial trade, and a relatively small negative list of sensitive items with no or limited duty concessions), services, investment and identified areas of economic cooperation.

CECA with Singapore was implemented from August 1, 2005. The Agreement on South Asia Free Trade Area (SAFTA) was signed by member countries of South Asian

Association for Regional Cooperation (SAARC) in January, 2004. Negotiation on all aspects of SAFTA was concluded and the tariff liberalization programme was implemented from July 1, 2006.

Framework Agreement on Comprehensive Economic Cooperation between ASEAN and India, Framework Agreement for Bangladesh, India, Myanmar, Sri Lanka and Thailand Economic Cooperation (BIMSTEC) FTA, and India-Thailand Framework Agreement have also been signed, and FTA on goods, services and investment with BIMSTEC is under negotiation. India-China, India-Japan, and India-South Korea joint study groups have also been set up.

South Asia Free Trade Area (SAFTA)

The Agreement on SAFTA was signed during the 12th SAARC Summit on January 6, 2004 in Islamabad. The tariff liberalisation programme under the Agreement came into force from July 1, 2006. India, Pakistan and Sri Lanka are categorized as non-least developed contracting states (NLDCS) and Bangladesh, Bhutan, Maldives and Nepal are categorized as least developed contracting states (LDCS).

Afghanistan which became the eighth member of SAARC during the 14th SAARC Summit held on April 3-4, 2007 in New Delhi would become a party to the SAFTA Agreement as an LDC member.

Article 7 of the SAFTA Agreement provides for a phased tariff liberalization programme (TLP) under which, in two years, NLDCS would bring down tariffs to 20 percent, while LDCS will bring them down to 30 percent. Non-LDCS will then bring down tariffs from 20 percent to 0-5 percent in 5 years (Sri Lanka, 6 years), while LDCS will do so in 8 years. NLDCs will reduce their tariffs for LDC products to 0-5 percent in 3 years. This TLP would cover all tariff lines except those kept in the sensitive list (negative list) by the member states.

The salient features of the four annexes of SAFTA

Agreement are as under.

Rules of Origin: For giving preferential access to the member countries under SAFTA, the goods shall have undergone substantial manufacturing process in the exporting countries.

The substantial manufacturing process are defined in terms of twin criteria of change of tariff heading (CTH) at four-digit harmonized coding system (HS) and value content of 40 percent (30 percent for LDCSs).

Apart from the general rules, to provide for product specific rules (PSR) for 191 tariff lines to accommodate the interest of LDCSs, given their limited base for natural resources and undiversified industrial structure. The product specific rules have been provided clearly on technical grounds i.e. where both inputs and outputs are at the same four-digit HS level.

Mechanism for Compensation of Revenue Loss (MCRL) for the Least Developed Contracting States: The compensation to LDCSs, except to Maldives, would be available for four years; to Maldives it would be for six years. The MCRL to Afghanistan will also be at par with Maldives.

The compensation would be in the form of grant in US dollar. The compensation shall be subject to a cap of 1 percent of customs revenue collected on non-sensitive items under bilateral trade in the base year, i.e. average of 2004 and 2005. The compensation shall be administered by the SAFTA Committee of Experts as per the administrative arrangements.

Technical Assistance to Least Developed Contracting States in Agreed Areas: The main areas covered are capacity building in standards, product certification, training of human resources, data management, institutional upgradations, improvement of legal systems and administration, customs procedures and trade facilitation, market development and promotion.

Implementation of SAFTA Agreement: Tariff concessions granted under the SAARC Preferential Trading

Arrangement (SAPTA) would cease for the LDC member states once the Non-LDCSs complete the trade liberalization programme (TLP) for LDCSs within three years. If any items, on which SAPTA concessions are available to LDCSs, appear in the sensitive list of Non-LDCSs, they shall maintain the same level of concessions through derogation under Article 7(3)(a) and indicate the same in their respective sensitive lists, and if the items under TLP enjoy tariff preferences under SAPTA, the Non-LDCS shall reduce their tariff on those items to a rate not higher than the rate applicable for LDCS under SAPTA on the date agreed for base rate for TLP.

The base rate for the purpose of tariff reduction would be MFN applied rate existing as on January 1, 2006.

The TLP became operational from July 1, 2006 with the condition that the TLP for the first two years would be completed by December 31, 2007, i.e. within two years of SAFTA coming into force.

India, with a view to providing greater market access to its neighbouring least developed countries, unilaterally reduced tariffs to zero percent for LDCS countries of SAFTA with effect from January 1, 2008 thereby completing the SAFTA tariff liberalization for these countries one year ahead of December 31, 2008 stipulated in the SAFTA Agreement. The notifications issued by Pakistan for SAFTA tariff concessions have an India specific-rider that Indian imports into Pakistan would continue to be as per their positive list of importable items from India.

India and ASEAN

India's engagement with the Association of Southeast Asian Nations (ASEAN) started with its *Look East Policy* in the year 1991. ASEAN has a membership of 10 countries, namely Brunei Darussalam, Cambodia, Indonesia, Lao PDR, Malaysia, Myanmar, Philippines, Singapore, Thailand and Vietnam. India became a sectoral dialogue partner of ASEAN in 1992 and full dialogue partner in 1996. In November 2001, the ASEAN-India relationship was upgraded to the summit level.

The 1st ASEAN Economic Ministers (AEM)-India Consultations were held on 15th September 2002 in Brunei Darussalam where the Ministers, after discussing the joint study report decided to establish an ASEAN-India Economic Linkages Task Force (AIELTF). The AIELTF was asked to prepare a draft framework agreement to enhance the ASEAN-India trade and economic cooperation before the 2nd AEM-India Consultations. Subsequently, at the First ASEAN-India Summit held on November 5, 2002 in Phnom Penh, Cambodia, the Prime Minister of India made the following major announcements:

- India will extend special and differential trade treatment to ASEAN countries, based on their levels of development to improve their market access to India.
- FTA within 10 years timeframe.

A framework agreement on comprehensive economic cooperation between the Association of South East Asian Nations (ASEAN) and India was signed by the Prime Minster of India and the heads of nation/governments of ASEAN members during the Second ASEAN-India Summit on October 8, 2003 in Bali, Indonesia.

The key elements of the Framework Agreement on Comprehensive Economic Cooperation between ASEAN and India covered FTA in goods, services and investment, as well as areas of economic cooperation. The Agreement also provided for an early harvest programme (EHP) which covers areas of economic cooperation and a common list of items for exchange of tariff concessions as a confidence building measure.

Presently, the ASEAN-India Trade Negotiating Committee (TNC) is undertaking negotiations for a comprehensive economic cooperation agreement (CECA) which includes a free trade area in goods, services and investment. Agreement has been reached on the rules of origin and dispute settlement mechanism. The TNC is now negotiating the modalities for tariff reduction and elimination.

On August 13, 2009, India and ASEAN signed the trade in goods agreement under the broader framework of a Comprehensive Economic Cooperation Agreement (CECA) between India and ASEAN. The trade in goods agreement provides for elimination of basic customs duty on 80 percent of the tariff lines accounting for 75 percent of the trade in a gradual manner starting from January 1, 2010. India has excluded 489 HS 6 digit lines from the list of tariff concessions and 590 HS 6 digit lines from the list of tariff eliminations to address sensitivities in agriculture, textiles, chemicals, etc. Conclusion of negotiations on Agreement on Services and Investment was announced on December 20, 2012. The cabinet approved and ratified the agreements on December 19, 2013.

India-Sri Lanka Free Trade Agreement (ISLFTA)

India-Sri Lanka Free Trade Agreement, signed in December 1998 and in operation since March 2000, provides for tariff reduction/elimination in a phased manner on all items except the negative list and tariff rate quota (TRQ) items. While India has already completed the tariff elimination programme in March 2003, Sri Lanka was scheduled to reach zero duty by 2008.

Now, both sides are in advanced stage of negotiation on having a Comprehensive Economic Partnership Agreement (CEPA) which would encompass trade in goods as well as trade in services and economic cooperation.

India-Thailand Comprehensive Economic Cooperation Agreement (CECA)

In November 2001, the Prime Minister of Thailand, Dr. Thaksin Shinawatra and the Prime Minister of India agreed to set up a joint working group (JWG) to undertake feasibility study on a free trade agreement between India and Thailand.

The joint working group observed that the present policy regimes in both the countries were conducive to more intensive bilateral economic integration and a free trade agreement could prove to be a building block for other sub-regional, regional and global economic integration processes of which both countries are a part. Having observed rich potential of trade expansion, the study concluded that the proposed free trade agreement between India and Thailand is feasible, desirable and mutually beneficial. Accordingly, a joint negotiating group was set up to draft the framework agreement on India-Thailand FTA.

During the visit of Indian Prime Minister to Thailand, a framework agreement for establishing free trade between India and Thailand was signed by the commerce ministers of the two sides on October 9, 2003 in Bangkok, Thailand. The framework agreement covers FTA in goods, services and investment and areas of economic cooperation. The framework agreement also provided for an early harvest scheme (EHS) under which 82 common items of export interest to the sides have been agreed for elimination of tariff on a fast track basis.

The tariff concessions on 82 items of EHS list began from September 1, 2004. The tariffs on these items became zero for both sides from September 1, 2006. As on date, the early harvest scheme on 82 items has been implemented.

India-Thailand Trade Negotiating Committee (TNC) has been constituted and discussions are being held on the text of FTA, rules of origin, dispute settlement mechanism and sensitive list. 17 rounds of negotiations for FTA in goods have so far been held. The 29th round of Trade Negotiating Committee scheduled for December 16-18, 2013 was cancelled by Thailand on account of internal disturbances.

Bay of Bengal Initiative for Multi-Sectoral Technical and Economic Cooperation (BIMSTEC) Free Trade Agreement (FTA)

The initiative to establish Bangladesh-India-Sri Lanka-Thailand Economic Cooperation (BIST-EC) was taken by

Thailand in 1994 to explore economic cooperation on a sub-regional basis involving contiguous countries of Southeast and South Asia grouped around the Bay of Bengal. Myanmar was admitted in December 1997 and the initiative was renamed as BIMSTEC. It may be mentioned that the initiative involves 3 members of SAARC (India, Bangladesh and Sri Lanka) and 2 members of ASEAN (Thailand, Myanmar). BIMSTEC is visualized as a *bridging link* between two major regional groupings, i.e. ASEAN and SAARC. BIMSTEC is an important element in India's *Look East* strategy and adds a new dimension to our economic cooperation with Southeast Asian countries.

The 2nd BIMSTEC Summit was held on November 13, 2008 in New Delhi, India. The Summit took place four years after the 1st BIMSTEC Summit in Thailand.

In conclusion, the leaders expressed their satisfaction at the progress that has been made in the negotiations for a Free Trade Agreement in trade in goods and called for their early conclusion. They welcomed the establishment of the centres for energy and weather and climate in India and the BIMSTEC Cultural Observatory in Bhutan. They also expressed concern at the threat which terrorism poses to the region and satisfaction with the finalization of the BIMSTEC Convention on Combating International Terrorism, Transnational Organized Crime and Illicit Drug Trafficking.

India-Singapore Comprehensive Economic Cooperation Agreement (CECA)

A Joint Study Group (JSG) for establishing a Comprehensive Economic Cooperation Agreement (CECA) between the two countries was set up on April 8, 2002. The JSG submitted its report on April 8, 2003.

The JSG identified areas of increased economic engagement between the two countries and also recommended measures to be taken. The JSG recommended the early launching of negotiations for a CECA to be structured as an integrated package of agreement between India and Singapore including the following:

1. A free trade agreement, which would include, *inter alia*, trade in goods and services and investment.
2. A bilateral agreement on investment promotion, protection and cooperation.
3. An improved double taxation avoidance agreement.
4. A more liberal Air Services Agreement and Open Skies for Charter Flights.
5. A work programme of cooperation in a number of areas including health care, education, media, tourism and the creation.

'Declaration of Intent' was signed between the two countries on April 8, 2003. Negotiations on CECA were launched in New Delhi on May 27-28, 2003.

The Comprehensive Economic Cooperation Agreement (CECA) between India and Singapore was signed on June 29, 2005 by the Prime Minister Manmohan Singh and Mr. Lee Hsien Loong, Prime Minister of Singapore. The CECA has become operational with effect from August 1, 2005. In December 2007, India granted market access on additional 539 tariff lines through a Protocol amending the India-Singapore CECA.

The implementation of CECA is reviewed regularly at the level of Secretaries. The 2nd review of India-Singapore CECA was launched by the Commerce and Industry Minister, India on May 11, 2010. The 1st secretary level meeting of the 2nd review was held in Singapore on 3rd August, 2010. Thereafter, Working Group meetings on goods and services and investment were held time to time, with the last meeting held in Singapore in September 2011.

Asia-Pacific Trade Agreement (APTA)

The Asia-Pacific Trade Agreement (APTA), previously named the Bangkok Agreement, signed in 1975 as an initiative of ESCAP, is a preferential tariff arrangement that aims at promoting intra-regional trade through exchange of mutually agreed concessions by member countries. APTA has 7 members, namely Bangladesh, China, India, Republic of Korea, Lao People's Democratic Republic, Sri Lanka and Mongolia (acceded in 2013). ESCAP functions as the secretariat for the agreement.

The second ministerial council meeting of APTA was held in Goa on October 26, 2007. The important decisions taken in the meeting were as follows:

1. An announcement to launch the 4th round of negotiations was made. The standing committee has been directed to conclude the negotiations by the 3rd ministerial council meeting.
2. The standing committee is to adopt modalities for extension of negotiations in other areas such as non-tariff measures, trade facilitation, services, and investment. To this effect the prospects of APTA have been widen by the Ministers.
3. A common set of operational procedures for the certificate and verification of the origin of goods for APTA was approved and it was decided that the same would be implemented w.e.f. January 1, 2008.
4. The standing committee and the secretariat would take necessary action to expand the membership of this agreement and member countries to give positive consideration to support the secretariat's activities relating to APTA.

To move forward the 4th round of negotiations, the APTA sub-regional seminar on February 24, 2009 and 31st session of the standing committee were held on February 25-27, 2009 in Bangkok. The third meeting of the ministerial council and the 35th session of the standing committee were held on December 15, 2009 and December 13-14, 2010 respectively in Seoul, South Korea.

India-Chile Preferential Trade Agreement (PTA)

A framework agreement to promote economic cooperation

between India and Chile was signed on January 20, 2005. The framework agreement envisaged a preferential trade agreement (PTA) between the two countries as a first step. The framework agreement also provides for a joint study group to go into the issues relating to a free trade agreement between the two sides.

As a follow up to the framework agreement, a PTA was finalized after five rounds of negotiations between the two sides. Official-level meeting was held in February 2014 to discuss the issues of the India-Chile PTA. The PTA has two annexes relating to the list of products on which the two sides have agreed to give fixed tariff preferences to each other and three annexes relating to the rules of origin, preferential safeguard measures and dispute settlement procedures.

The framework agreement to promote economic cooperation, signed between India and Chile on January 20, 2005, provided for a joint study group (JSG) to identify the potential for cooperation between the two sides in trade in goods and services, investments and other areas of economic cooperation. The terms of reference for the JSG were finalized during the negotiations held with Chile in June 2005. The Chilean side submitted a draft report of its part of the JSG recommending the feasibility of an FTA between India and Chile.

First meeting of the joint study group was held during the PTA negotiations in November 2005. The draft reports prepared by Chile and India were discussed during the meeting. Both sides agreed to submit their conclusions and recommendations to their governments for guiding further action on the matter.

India-South Korea Comprehensive Economic Partnership Agreement (CEPA)

On October 6, 2004, India and South Korea agreed to establish a joint study group to take a comprehensive view of bilateral economic linkages between the two countries. In particular, the joint study group (JSG) was mandated with the task of examining the feasibility of a Comprehensive Economic Partnership Agreement (CEPA) between the two countries.

The JSG, composed of Government officials, economists and representatives of business communities of South Korea and India, concluded that a CEPA between Korea and India would provide significant benefits for both countries.

The JSG recommended that the South Korea-India CEPA should cover, among other things:

1. Trade in goods.
2. Trade in services.
3. Measures for trade facilitations.
4. Promotion, facilitation and liberalization of investment flows.
5. Measures for promoting bilateral economic cooperation in identified sectors.

In pursuance to the recommendations of JSG, a joint task force (JTF) composed of government officials was constituted. Negotiations for a Comprehensive Economic Partnership Agreement between India and Korea commenced on March 23, 2006, and were substantially concluded in the 12th meeting of the joint task force (JTF) held during September 22-25, 2008 in Seoul.

An India-South Korea CEPA was signed on August 6, 2009 and implemented with effect from January 1, 2010 covering trade in goods, investment, services and bilateral cooperation in areas of common interest. Under the CEPA, tariffs will be reduced or eliminated on 93 percent of Korea's tariff lines and 85 percent of India's tariff lines. It will facilitate trade in services through additional commitments made by both countries to ease movement of independent professional and contractual service suppliers.

India-Gulf Cooperation Council (GCC) Free Trade Agreement (FTA)

The Gulf Co-operation Council (GCC) is a customs union

comprising of Bahrain, Kuwait, Oman, Qatar, Saudi Arabia and United Arab Emirates. They are India's third largest trading partners, with exports to this region constituting about 3-4 percent of India's global exports and our imports from this region accounting for over 20 percent of India's global imports.

India is in the process of negotiating a free trade agreement with GCC and the first round of negotiation was held on March 21-22, 2006. Trade in services and investment cooperation as well as general economic cooperation is proposed to be synergized with the FTA.

India-Japan Comprehensive Economic Cooperation Agreement (CECA)

During the visit of Prime Minister Koizumi of Japan to India in April 2005, the Prime Ministers of the two countries directed that the India-Japan joint study group (JSG), be launched by June 2005, to submit its report within a year, focusing on measures required for a comprehensive expansion of trade in goods, trade in services, investment flows and other areas of economic relations between the two countries.

JSG was constituted to focus on measures required for comprehensive expansion of trade in good, trade in services, investment flows and other areas of economic relations between the two countries. The JSG finalized its report which was submitted to the two Prime Ministers at St. Petersburg on July 17, 2006. The JSG recommended that the Governments of Japan and India launch an inter-governmental negotiation to develop an economic partnership agreement (EPA)/comprehensive economic partnership agreement (CEPA), within a reasonable period of time. The EPA/CEPA needs to be consistent with WTO provisions, while sensitive sectors should be treated with flexibility and practicality. The JSG also recommended that negotiations on the proposed EPA/CEPA be conducted in a specially-constituted joint task force (JTF), or another mutually agreed suitable mechanism, consisting of government officials. The JTF may consult with the representatives of the business community whenever necessary.

A joint ministerial statement on the launching of a JTF to develop an economic partnership agreement (EPA)/ comprehensive partnership agreement (CEPA) between India and Japan was issued on December 15, 2006 during the Prime Minister's visit to Japan. As per the negotiating structure annexed to the joint ministerial statement the EPA/CEPA negotiations consist of meetings at the chief delegate level and the working level.

Eleven meetings of the JTF have been held so far (four at chief delegate level and seven at the working level). In the fifth meeting of the JTF held during January 8-11, 2008, in India, both sides agreed to the modalities of negotiations on market access of trade in goods.

On investment, IPR, trade in services, custom procedure and other related issues various groups have been constituted for negotiations.

An in principle Agreement was signed during the 14th Round on September 9, 2010 in Tokyo.

India-Malaysia Comprehensive Economic Cooperation Agreement (CECA)

On December 20, 2004, the Prime Ministers of Malaysia and India agreed to the setting up of a joint study group (JSG) to explore the feasibility of Comprehensive Economic Cooperation Agreement (CECA) between the two countries. In accordance with the mandate granted by the two Prime Ministers, the JSG was duly constituted in March 2005.

The JSG Report was submitted in January 2007 and adopted by both the governments on August 11, 2007.

India-Malaysia CECA negotiations were launched in February 2008. The negotiations were concluded in September 2010. The CECA—including trade in goods, services, investment, and other areas of economic cooperation—would be signed as a single undertaking.

Taking into account the India-ASEAN Trade in Goods Agreement that was implemented in January 2010 between India and Malaysia, both sides have offered 'ASEAN+' market access in goods. On October 27, 2010, Prime Ministers of India and Malaysia announced conclusion of the negotiations with the Agreement scheduled to be signed by early 2011 and implemented by July 1, 2011.

India-Mauritius Comprehensive Economic Cooperation and Partnership Agreement (CECPA)

A joint study group (JSG) constituted in November 2003 to study the modalities of the CECPA discussed in detail the complementariness and potential synergies between the two economies and, in its report of November 2004, identified investment, trade in goods and services and general economic cooperation for developing modalities of CECPA.

During his visit to Mauritius from March 30-April 2, 2005, the Prime Minister of India conveyed India's acceptance of the report by the JSG on Comprehensive Economic Cooperation and Partnership Agreement and both sides agreed to set up a high-powered negotiating team for processing and finalizing the recommendations of this report within a twelve-month period. Accordingly, an empowered team was constituted for negotiating a Comprehensive Economic Cooperation and Partnership Agreement (CECPA) with Mauritius. Five rounds of talks have so far been held by the empowered team.

Texts of preferential trade agreement (PTA) and its annexures, viz. rules of origin, operational certification procedures and trade defence measures have been finalised.

The following MoUs/agreements were signed by India and Mauritius in October 2005 under the aegis of CECPA.

1. MoU in the field of consumer protection and legal metrology.
2. MoU between Bureau of Indian Standards (BIS) and Mauritius Standards Bureau (MSB).
3. MoU between Indian Institute of Public Administration

(IIPA) and Government of Mauritius.

4. MoU on preferential trade agreement (PTA).

Negotiations are being held on the liberalization of trade in services with a view to creating a more liberal, facilitative, transparent and competitive services regime in the two countries and to strengthen cooperation in services sector.

Issues relating to financial services sector, mutual recognition agreements and movement of natural persons are being deliberated upon. Both sides have agreed to explore the possibility of expanding trade in services by synergizing with the Common Market for Eastern and Southern Africa (COMESA) and Southern African Development Community (SADC) markets.

Issues relating to improving the effectiveness of the existing double taxation avoidance agreement for the mutual benefit of the two countries and review of the existing bilateral investment protection agreement to enhance its scope and effectiveness are being deliberated upon. Discussions have been held for improving the existing legal framework in both countries in this regard and other issues related to facilitation of investment.

Cooperation in the fields of health, standards, SMEs development, education, information technology and telecommunication, seafood industry and cooperation between private sectors of the two countries have been deliberated upon for investment, capacity building, training, technology transfer and related activities.

India-SACU Preferential Trade Agreement (PTA) Negotiations

South Africa, Lesotho, Swaziland, Botswana and Namibia have formed the South Africa Customs Union (SACU) with a common custom tariff policy. A joint working group (JWG) consisting of Government representatives from both sides was set up to examine the proposal to prepare a draft framework treaty for the preferential trade agreement (PTA) between

India and SACU countries. In a meeting of JWG held in Namibia on September 6-7, 2004, the draft framework agreement was finalized.

The sixth session of the India-South Africa Joint Ministerial Commission Meeting was held in New Delhi on December 5-6, 2005. Both sides agreed that a comprehensive free trade agreement within a reasonable time and in the interim, a limited scope agreement providing for exchange of tariff concessions on select list of products, between India and SACU would give further impetus to bilateral trade and urged its early conclusion.

India-Pakistan Trading Arrangement

India and Pakistan have no formal trade agreement. India has granted most favoured nation (MFN) status to Pakistan, whereas Pakistan maintains a list of importable items from India called 'positive list' which now consists of 1,938 items.

Both countries had constituted a joint study group (JSG) at the level of commerce secretary. Its first meeting was held in February 2005 and the last (third meeting) in New Delhi on August 2, 2007. In this meeting both sides are in the process of discussions to address the issues concerning customs cooperation, sanitary, phyto-sanitary measures and technical barriers to trade, standards and conformance to the extent feasible.

Apart from the JSG, the issues pertaining to commercial and economic cooperation are also discussed at commerce secretary level within the framework of the composite dialogue. The fourth round of dialogue was held in New Delhi on July 31-August 1, 2007.

Bilateral trade and commerce talks were held between commerce secretaries of India and Pakistan on April 27-28, 2011 in Islamabad. The two sides, *inter alia*, agreed to improve trade infrastructure and expand trade through Attari-Wagah land route. Both sides agreed to undertake new initiatives to enable trade in electricity and Bt. Cotton seeds as also expand trade in petroleum products.

It was agreed that cooperation in information technology sector would be encouraged through the private sector. Both sides agreed to facilitate grant of business visas to encourage expansion of trade. Pakistan recognized that grant of MFN status to India would help in expanding bilateral trade relations. It agreed to replace its present 'positive list' with 'negative list'.

India-Nepal Treaty of Trade

Treaty of Trade: The bilateral trade between India and Nepal is regulated by the treaty of trade. The current treaty was to in force for a period of 5 years with effect from March 6, 2002. The treaty was to expire on March 6, 2007. Hence, both Governments of Nepal and India decided to renew the treaty in its current form with effect from March 6, 2007.

Both sides are also engaged in mutual consultation process to amend the treaty of trade and once this process is over, the amended treaty of trade shall replace the existing treaty, after necessary approval. Pending completion of the process for its renewal with certain amendments proposed, the validity of the agreement would continue till a new treaty comes into force.

Under this treaty, there is free trade on mutually agreed to primary products from each other as indicated in protocol to Article IV of the treaty. In the case of industrial goods produced in Nepal, Article V of the treaty provides for India to give, on a non-reciprocal basis, duty-free access to Nepalese goods without any quantity restriction. This is subject to fulfilling the twin criterion of four-digit tariff head change and value addition of 30 percent at ex-factory price in Nepal. This duty-free access is, however, restricted to annual quotas on four sensitive items in the interest of the domestic industries in these sectors. These are vanaspati (1,00,000 metric tones), copper products and acrylic yarn (10,000 metric tones each) and zinc oxide (2,500 metric tones). The routes for bilateral trade can be mutually decided; in the present treaty, 22 mutually agreed routes are prescribed for bilateral trade. The treaty provides for setting up joint committee in the event the imports under the treaty results in injury to the domestic industry in each country.

Treaty of Transit: India provides transit facilities to the landlocked Nepal under the treaty of transit. The current treaty which was renewed in January 2006 would be in force for a period of seven years up to January 5, 2013. This treaty provides for free movement of traffic-in-transit across territories of each other through mutually agreed routes for trade with third countries subject to taking measures to ensure that this does not infringe legitimate interests/security interests of each other. Traffic in transit is exempted from customs/all transit duties. The treaty provides for exit/entry points as may be mutually agreed upon. India has allowed 15 transit routes to Nepal but so far not availed of this facility from Nepal. Merchant ships of Nepal are accorded treatment no less favourable than that accorded to ships of any other foreign country. Presently, Kolkata/Haldia are the operational entry points for Nepal's trade with third countries. Nepal has requested for similar facilities at Mumbai and Kandla.

Agreement of Cooperation to Control Unauthorized Trade: India and Nepal have also signed an agreement of cooperation to control unauthorized trade between the two countries. This agreement was last renewed for 5 years with effect from March 6, 2007. The objective of this agreement is to check illegal trade (smuggling) between the two countries.

Inter-Governmental Committee (IGC) at Commerce Secretary-Level: Both countries have established a forum known as Inter- Governmental Committee at commerce secretary-level to address the problems relating to bilateral trade, transit facilities and prevention of unauthorized trade which meet as often as required.

India-EU Broad-based Trade and Investment Agreement

On June 28, 2007, India and the EU began negotiations on

a broad-based Bilateral Trade and Investment Agreement (BTIA) in Brussels, Belgium.

These negotiations are pursuant to the commitment made by political leaders at the India-EU Summit held in Helsinki on October 13, 2006 to move towards negotiations for a broad-based trade and investment agreement. India and the EU expect to promote bilateral trade by removing barriers to trade in goods and services and investment across all sectors of the economy. Both parties believe that a comprehensive and ambitious agreement that is consistent with WTO rules and principles would open new markets and would expand opportunities for Indian and EU businesses. The negotiations cover trade in goods, trade in services, investment, sanitary and phyto-sanitary measures, technical barriers to trade, rules of origin, trade facilitation and customs cooperation, competition, trade defence mechanism, government procurement, dispute settlement, IPR and GIs.

Fifteen rounds of negotiations and a number of inter-sessional meetings have been held till date. A ministerial review meeting was held on April 15, 2013 at Brussels.

12

Uruguay Round of Multilateral Trade Negotiations and India

The Uruguay Round of Multilateral Trade Negotiations (MTNs) was launched at Punta del Este in Uruguay in 1986 at the ministerial level GATT meeting. The main objective of GATT meetings was to expand international trade, and remove obstacles to the free flow of trade between nations. The Uruguay Round was the eighth in the GATT series of negotiations. Some other well-known rounds were the Kennedy Round and the Tokyo Round.

The Uruguay Round covered a much wider ambit of issues than MTNs. There were two simultaneous tracks, than earlier MTNs. There are two simultaneous tracks of negotiations GNG (Group of Negotiations on Goods) and GNS (Group of Negotiations on Services). In fact, its was the first time that services were brought in, mainly on the insistence of the United States which had the most to gain from their inclusion.

The GNG covered fourteen areas related to trade in goods. These included: (i) tariffs, (ii) non-tariff barriers (NTBs), (iii) products, (iv) natural resource-based products, (v) textiles and clothing, (vi) agriculture, (vii) GATT articles, (viii) safeguards, (ix) MTN agreements and arrangements, (x) subsidies and countervailing measures, (xi) dispute settlement, (xii) Trade-related Investment Measures (TRIMS), and (xiii) Trade-related Intellectual Property Rights (TRIPS). The TRIPS negotiations included trade in counterfeit goods and to develop a multilateral framework of principles, rules and disciplines dealing with international trade in counterfeit goods. The negotiations must also develop effective and adequate protection of intellectual property rights. These negotiations were to examine existing GATT articles on trade restricting and distorting effects of investment measures and develop further provisions to prevent such adverse effects, and the functioning of the GATT System. A GNS was simultaneously established to oversee negotiations on liberalising trade in services. The objective was to expand trade in services under the conditions of transparency and liberalisation.

The Uruguay Round was scheduled to be completed by 1990 i.e. within four years after commencement. However, even after seven years, that is 1993, the negotiations still did not conclude. It was this stalemate that prompted an intervention by the Director General of GATT, Mr. Arthur Dunkel to break the deadlock on contentious issues...it was called the Dunkel Draft or Dunkel Package, also derisively called DDT (Dunkel Draft Treaty).

Dunkel Proposals

We will now discuss some of the Dunkel proposals. We will first discuss the reintegration of textiles into the GATT framework. Trade in textiles and clothing was governed by the multi fibre agreement (MFA) in force since 1974. Third World countries which were large exporters of textiles faced quotas imposed under MFA. The Dunkel Draft proposed a phasing out of these quotas over a period of ten years. After a fresh agreement enters into force (say in 1994), 16 percent of the textile sector would be integrated into GATT, with larger shares being integrated each year. However, the definition of textiles itself was widened to cover a larger range of products.

Negotiations on trade-disorienting agricultural policies were stalled for several months due to differences between the European Community (EC) and the US over farm subsidies. Studies have shown that there will be substantial gains once agricultural trade is liberalised. The contentious issue is the heavy subsidy given by the EC countries for production and export of basic agricultural foodstuffs. The Dunkel proposals called for reduction in domestic and export subsidies; and replacement of non-tariff barriers, like quotas and quantitative restrictions by tariffs. The deadlock between the US and EC appeared to have been resolved with the two reaching agreement (The Blair House Accord) on contentious issues. However, France reneged under pressure from its farmers and the whole accord was in jeopardy.

Some Third World countries argued that government measures to encourage agricultural and rural development form an integral part of the development programmes, and should, therefore, not come under the purview of GATT. The Dunkel Draft does have preferential treatment for LDCs with regard to agriculture. All investment subsidies were given an across-the board exemption and input subsidies to low income producers were also exempted.

In the negotiations on TRIMS, there were differences among the developed countries, and the third world with regard to the export obligations imposed on industries. LDCs argued that export commitments do not inhibit trade. Most of the policies with regard to TRIMS would be acceptable to third world countries. There were no clear-cut proposals regarding foreign direct investment (FDI) in the Dunkel Draft.

With regard to services, doubts were expressed by Brazil and India, that the Third World countries would be swamped by banking and insurance firms from the advanced countries. Also, the LDCs would not be able to contribute much in those services where they have a comparative advantage i.e. those involving labour (like construction, computer programming), since the movement of people across borders would not be permitted.

After initial dithering, the possibility of an agreement on services was nevertheless in sight. Rules regarding transparency of regulations, most favoured nation (MFN) treatment, maintenance of safeguards and liberalisation in stages will apply uniformly to all kinds of services, including labour-rclated services.

Intellectual Property Rights

We next come to TRIPS (Trade-related Intellectual Property Rights) where the Dunkel proposals demanded a lot of changes in intellectual property protection from India and other Third World countries. TRIPS is an area where the Dunkel proposals demanded most concessions from India, which recognises only process patents not product patents for pharmaceutical and agricultural products, and limits patents to 14 years or 7 years from the time the patent was applied for. India would also have liked to retain flexibility for excluding vital areas like pharmaceuticals, chemicals and food technology from product patents.

The Dunkel proposals required tougher enforcement of copyrights and trade marks by India. It required a change in Indian legislation on patents to make it conform to the Paris Convention. Apart from animal varieties, plant varieties and biological processes, product patents have immediately to be granted in all other areas. In so far as only process patents continue during a transitional period, the burden of proof will be reversed and placed on the defendant. The term of the patents will be increased to 20 years.

Intellectual property and its protection was the most contentious issue in the Uruguay Round. Human being is gifted with the quality of thinking and is forever trying to find solutions to problems. New ideas and inventions keep on emerging in science and technology. Similarly, new creations are made in the field of art and literature. All this is the outcome of human intelligence. The resulting outcome is known as intellectual property. Intellectual property is thus the creation of the human mind, the human intellect. Intellectual property is created by incorporating information in tangible objects capable of being multiplied in unlimited number of times anywhere in the world. The property is basically in the concept, incorporated in an actual product or process. Intellectual property is usually divided into two branches: (a) patents, designs and trade marks, which are also termed 'industrial property', and (b) copyrights. It is customary to distinguish between inventions that consist of products and inventions that consist of processes. There may also be a combination of both.

Thus, there could be a product patent, a process patent or a product and process patent. A new process or an improved process could be a good subject matter for a patent; however to be patentable, a process must lead to some result.

India is governed by the Indian Patents Act of 1970. If this is altered in consonance with the Paris Convention, the nascent indigenous pharmaceutical industry will be destroyed; research efforts in process development would be dampened and drug prices would be pushed up enormously.

Let it be noted that nations which signed the Paris Convention in the last century were all Western nations. The period when the Convention was signed saw a spate of inventions in a variety of fields in Europe. The Berne Convention was for protecting copyrights of authors, and artists while the Paris Convention dealt with wider issues.

Negotiations on TRIPS began in March 1987. Developed countries, by and large, have supported a comprehensive package on TRIPS. This package would be under GATT and would encompass substantive standards of protection for all areas of intellectual property (patents, trademarks, copyrights), effective enforcement measures (both at the border and internally) and effective dispute settlement provisions. In addition to a draft legal text submitted by the US, other legal texts also have been submitted by the EC, Switzerland and Japan.

Most developed countries desire a straight-forward application of GATT to the standards for copyright protection set out in the Berne Convention for the protection of literary and artistic works.

The polarization of views between developed and developing countries is sharper. The popular impression of TRIPS in developed countries is that it is all a matter of piracy and counterfeiting. But there is more to TRIPS than that. LDCs are genuinely concerned about patent protection for technologically sophisticated but vitally important goods like drugs, chemical fertilizers, and plant hybrids. LDCs have major technological and public interest objectives to consider. India would like to retain the flexibility for excluding vital areas like pharmaceuticals, plant hybrids and food technology from product patents. The patent system is also important for promoting industrial development, as is the mechanism of compulsory licensing of a new product. Besides, India and 14 other LDCs feel that GATT involvement should be limited to broader measures to address copyright piracy and trademark counterfeiting. There should be flexibility in national laws on TRIPS in accordance with developmental objectives. Apart from piracy and counterfeiting, guidelines in other areas like substantive standards should be administered outside GATT, possibly through the World Intellectual Property Organization (WIPO).

Indian Position on GATT

The political leadership in India will have to firm up its views on matters of vital interest to India like TRIPS and textiles and agriculture. India will have to seek changes in the Dunkel Draft in five key areas. These are: (i) trade in textiles, (ii) agricultural trade liberalisation, (iii) rules governing anti-dumping, (iv) provisions on cross-retaliation, and (v) TRIPS.

Commerce ministry officials expressed that the patent stalemate in multilateral talks, owing to differences between leading industrialized nations on agricultural trade liberalisation has allowed India the necessary time to evolve its own stand.

At the same time, the government is keen on an early solution in the Uruguay Round of negotiations—for India has a high stake in the finalisation of a new multilateral trade agreement. The collapse of the round would only lead to the growth of protectionism in the industrialised countries, through the strengthening of regional trade blocks, to the detriment of LDCs like India.

In textiles, the improvements in the draft agreement that India will seek would be for a shorter period than 10 years, prescribed by Dunkel for phasing out protectionist MFA, and faster integration of the textile trade with the GATT framework by removing quota restrictions on a large number of items in the very initial years.

India sought seven specific improvements in the Dunkel proposals regarding agricultural trade liberalisation. These were the following:

1. Exemption from a commitment on reduction of subsidy on purchase of food so as to ensure food security. This means that India can continue to subsidise its buffer stock operations.
2. Enhancement for LDCs of the maximum percentage of subsidies for agricultural commodities from the 10 percent provided in the text, implying that agricultural subsidies can cross the ten percent ceiling to reasonable limits.
3. Exemption of input subsidies from the maximum limits prescribed for Indian farmers (at least those owning up to four hectares) for the purpose of calculating the aggregate measure of support (AMS).
4. Additional flexibility in regard to subsidies for crops grown on marginal land, implying special provisions for less productive agricultural land.
5. Adoption of a realistic period for enforcement of external price comparisons.
6. An exemption for LDCs from tarrification in respect of some basic food stuffs even after balance of payment problems are over, to safeguard against pronounced fluctuations.
7. Sharper reduction in export subsidy doled out to their farmers by developed countries, to protect interests of developing country farmers.

In the area of anti-dumping rules, India pressed for the

following provisions:

1. A threshold to be fixed for market penetration by the products of a country before anti-dumping duties can be levied against it.
2. A level of sales in the domestic market of the developing country which is considered adequate for the purpose of making price comparisons.
3. Immunity from anti-dumping investigations to suppliers who are already subject to quantitative restrictions.
4. A "sunset" clause for anti-dumping action so that protection for sunset industries in the developed countries is not provided.

A declaration from the developed countries that take recourse to cross-retaliation against LDCs only when the adverse effect of dumping or other violation is very great and a clear commitment on the repeal of domestic laws which authorise unilateral retaliation for economic reasons, are the two other improvements sought by India.

With regard to the Dunkel proposals on TRIPS, which have been the most controversial of all, the government tried to secure the following improvements:

1. A special compulsory licensing provision for food products and pharmaceuticals.
2. A clear commitment that imports will not be regarded as a "working" of the patents.
3. Special provisions recognising the primacy of public interest in LDCs with regard to patent protection.
4. Adequate safeguards for farmers against plant breeder's rights.

There has been very little difference of opinion on legal consequences of an acceptance of the Dunkel Text. The general opinion is that the Indian patent law would have to be overhauled. The difference of opinion is on the assessment of the economic implications of such a move.

One view is that the general level of prices of all medicines would increase five to ten times. However, the present estimate of the number of drugs sold in the country which are under patents is 15 percent. Most medicines which are widely used are not protected according to official sources. Such medicines should be unaffected.

Commerce ministry officials feel that it would be difficult to fix a term of patent protection on the basis of national criteria; and the period of 20 years has to be viewed against the background of the fact that it has international consensus. Also, in the case of drugs, it takes about eight to ten years to get marketing approval after the grant of a patent.

On the other hand, some studies have shown that global trade could gain up to US$ 120 billion a year with a successful GATT agreement and all would benefit from this. Again, the current draft agreement has many useful rules for the settlement of international trade disputes, protectionist use of technical standards, anti-dumping measures, countervailing duties and numerous other non-tariff barriers to trade. It also offers safeguards for intellectual property, which remains a subject of controversy in India, but which is perhaps the only way now left for India, to avert protracted and damaging international disputes over intellectual property rights.

Third World Perspectives

The absence of a global agreement on trade could mean each country, or group of countries would go their own way, most likely generating fierce competition and world wide disputes over trade. A country like India, on the verge of joining the global economy in a meaningful way, would probably find access to world markets very difficult without the help of GATT.

The US administration has congressional sanction under a special fast track legislation, by which international agreements can be negotiated without detailed congressional surveillance, only up to 1993 to clinch international trade deals. After that, the American legislature may re-open the whole issue for domestic debate.

It is maintained in India that the multilateral trading system sanctioned by GATT was status quoist, maintaining the pre-dominance and pre-eminence of the first world countries on the international economy. Hardly any efforts have been made to lessen the first world and the third world. The negotiations and discussions were all first world oriented. Thus, GATT has not taken into account the pivotal role played by MNCs in fostering the inequitable relations between the first and the third world. Thus, while the clauses dealing with trade and development remained on the agenda of successive rounds of negotiations, the constraints in meeting the requirements of GATT arising from the exploitation of the third world by MNCs, did not come in for consideration, let alone discussion, even in the Uruguay Round. Now on the contrary, paradoxically the issue under consideration is how to provide greater strength to the MNCs for exploiting third world market.

If the proposals in the Dunkel Draft on the new patent regime were accepted, there would be a serious impact on the availability of new products through ingenious efforts, on the prices of new products, which would be exorbitant. In particular, the consumer would suffer, as high prices would have to be paid for essential medicines. R and D activity would also be seriously jeopardised. The product patent regime will take away opportunities for developing innovative processes. Small and tiny enterprises may have to close down, and thus employment prospects will be jeopardised in the third world.

On the other hand, some maintain that the absence of product patents really kills serious research into new products in India. Companies prefer to take the easy way of making some small changes in the process. Thus, Indian creativity is crippled. Besides, a weak patent law takes away the monetary incentive to spend money on serious R and D since the product can easily be copied.

The TRIMS proposals will have adverse effects on opportunities for domestic industry. Foreign investors would be able to decide the level and extent of foreign equity holdings and also the industries in which they should invest, which would naturally be in consumer durables and simple technologies, yielding huge profits. Domestic industry will thus be seriously affected. At the same time, one must also remember that India cannot do without new technology and investment from abroad.

Subsidies will be reduced for agricultural products, cutting them down to 10 percent of the cost of production. This will have a deleterious impact on farmers. The PDS (public distribution system) will also have to be remodelled and revamped. There will be extensive intervention in the third world's policies for independent agricultural development. However, sooner or later agriculture would have to do without subsidies and all would then benefit.

If the services sector and banking and insurance are kept open to foreign financial institutions, savings will be diverted to foreign institutions. The weaker sections of society in the third world countries will be the worst sufferers in this dispensation. While this may be true, it is also true that the only way to improve the gross inefficiency of public sector financial institutions is to make them face competition from Indian and foreign companies. Any improvement in the functioning of public sector banks will have a multiplier effect on the whole of Indian business.

The third world countries by compromising in the GATT would have to face the combined pressure of the world's wealthiest and most powerful countries. The alternative is for a country to isolate itself. The "New World Order" has ominous implications for trade issues as well. Thus, Uruguay Round has crucial implications for the Third World.

Options for India

With around 40 percent of India's exports being accounted for by the United States and Europe, any denial of access to these two markets could result in a quick return to the near bankrupt balance of payments situation of 1991. And those, who believe that such considerations have little to do with farmers, will do well to remember that agricultural exports will also be hit, and so will the import of several commodities, including petroleum products, which are critical for the rural sector.

The emphasis on increasing market access, for instance, has been interpreted primarily as an instrument to prise open the Indian market. But it also helps Indian exporters gain access to more lucrative markets than the Indian one. And with a growing recognition that sustained growth in Indian agriculture will require increased farm exports, the Dunkel Draft may not as adversely affect farmers as the more militant farmers' associations would have us to believe.

Such benefits will have to be weighed against the costs of the Dunkel Draft. There has been considerable attention drawn to the adverse consequences of patenting plant varieties not just in immediate economic terms, but also in terms of its impact, in the long run, on the genetic resources of the Third World.

If the rejection of the Dunkel Draft is not a valid option, all that can be sought is that as many favourable changes as possible are incorporated in a final agreement, if and when one does come about. And India cannot hope for too many such changes either. Its negotiating strength has been reduced by the developing world being far less of a force today that it was when the Uruguay Round began in Punta del Este. Moreover, with wide divergencies among developing countries, India cannot expect to benefit from the regionalisation of world trade.

There has been very little debate on the specifics of the government's negotiating position on the Dunkel Draft. Indeed, the focus on the impossible demand for rejecting the entire draft has contributed to the governments' negotiating position being determined primarily by short-term considerations.

The current political uncertainty is also bound to make the

government more concerned with the immediate impact of a trade agreement rather than the costs of opting out, which will only become evident in the long-term. The less than comfortable balance of payments position is also likely to keep the focus on the short-term effects on trade.

In an atmosphere, where political attention is focused on non-economic issues, the chances of the negotiating position being determined by a bureaucratic problem solving approach, rather than a long-term vision, is even greater. It is thus, hardly surprising that official concern has been almost entirely concentrated on the impact on textiles and pharmaceuticals, both areas, where the Dunkel Draft can have an immediate effect.

In case the Government cannot get the developed countries to accept our demand for the exclusion of chemical products from the scope of patentability, then we must provide for the license of right, a form of compulsory license to manufacture, which alone gives full scope to the manufacturers to produce patented inventions after paying royalties to the patent holder. Without such a provision, the government would not be able to ensure the development of strong national companies and also keep the prices of drugs down.

Unfortunately, the government is willing to jettison this provision and is searching for a way out in the provision for compulsory licensing for non-commercial public use. It is not difficult to see that this cannot cover many products. Non-commercial public use implies production at government cost. Clearly, in India where health care is now largely in the private sector, the provision for non-commercial public use cannot cover many patented drugs.

The claim that by using price control mechanisms, the government will be able to make drugs available at cheap prices is also based on false premise. Thanks to import being treated as 'working' of the patent under the TRIPS agreement, most drugs will be imported from the patent holders who, in the absence of competition, will be free to charge monopoly prices. Only in those cases where the patent holder has established local production, will the government be able to intervene and regulate prices.

Similarly, the attention of the public is being diverted from the real issues as far as seeds are concerned. The attempt of the Ministry of Commerce has been to keep some ill-informed criticisms alive by reiterating that the government will not accept the patenting of seeds or the removal of the right of farmers to save seed. In fact close reading of the Dunkel Draft, shows that the right of farmers to save seeds was not threatened by the Dunkel proposals. Therefore, no brave fight is required to get the US to give assurances on the right of farmers to save seed.

However, the view that the failure of the Uruguay Round will have disastrous consequences for India is unduly pessimistic. Trade wars will not be a necessary consequence of failure of the Uruguay Round, since both the GATT treaty and organisation will continue under the provisions of the Tokyo Round, howsoever frayed it might have become. Trade anarchy is thus not inevitable and catastrophic prognosis is therefore uncalled for. The Dunkel proposals can by no means be described as uniformly advantageous to India. On the contrary, there are elements within them, which may have an adverse impact on Indian commerce. A comparison of the gains and losses if India signs the Dunkel Draft is called for. The Dunkel Draft should not be a 'take it' or 'leave it' agreement and India should sign the Draft only after its reservations are considered and hopefully incorporated.

References

Abrol, D., "The Government Trips", *The Economic Times*, 5th June, 1993.

Baru, S., "GATT: Winter of Discontent", *Economic and Political Weekly*, 7th January, 1989.

Debroy, B., "The Uruguay Round: Status Paper on Issues Relevant to Developing Countries", *Foreign Trade Review*, 26, No. 3, 1991.

Debroy, B., "The Uruguay Round and Dunkel Draft", *The Hindu*, 5th and 6th February, 1992.

Dhar, B., "GATT and the New Trade Discipline: Prospects for the Developing Countries", National Working Group on Patent Laws, New Delhi, 1992.

Keyela, B.K., "Dunkel Proposals on the New Patent System: Impact on India", National Working Group on Patent Laws, and New Delhi, 1992.

Pani, N., "Should Farmers Reject the Dunkel Draft?", *The Economic Times*, 18th January, 1993.

Patel, S.J., "The South and the GATT Negotiations on the Services Sector", Ahmedabad: Sardar Patel Institute of Economic and Social Research, 1992.

Ponkshe, S., "The Management of Intellectual Property", Bhate and Ponkshe, Pune: UBS Publications, 1991.

Whalley, J., "The Uruguay Round and Beyond", Macmillan, 1989.

13

India and World Trade Organization (WTO)

The WTO is the only international body dealing with the rules of trade between nations. At its heart are the WTO agreements, negotiated and signed by the bulk of the World's trading nations. The WTO was established in 1995, as part of the Uruguay Round of Trade Negotiations. The three main purposes of WTO are:

1. To help trade flow as freely as possible.
2. To provide a forum for trade negotiations.
3. To settle trade disputes.

GATT and WTO

For several decades, GATT (General Agreement on Tariffs and Trade) was applied on a provisional basis. It was a multilateral agreement containing rules relative to trade in goods, and although it operated like a permanent agreement, it was without a permanent institutional framework, and was serviced by an ad hoc secretariat. The WTO now provides a permanent institutional framework for the multilateral trading system, with its own secretariat. In addition, the WTO not only covers trade in goods, as the GATT rules did, but also trade in services, and trade-related aspects of IPRs (intellectual property rights). Also, the dispute settlement mechanism has been considerably strengthened in the WTO.

Objectives and Functions of WTO

In the preamble of the Marrakesh Agreement establishing the WTO, the parties to the agreement recognize certain objectives to which they wish to contribute through the multilateral trading system. It is recognized that member's relations in the field of trade and economic endeavour, should be conducted with a view to raising standards of living, ensuring full employment and a large and steadily growing volume of real income, and effective demand and expanding the production of and trade in goods and services, while allowing for the optimal use of the world's resources in accordance with the objectives of sustainable development. The WTO agreement also recognizes the need for "positive efforts" to ensure that LDCs and especially the least developed among them, secure a share in the growth in international trade commensurate with the needs of their economic development.

The main functions of the WTO are:

1. To administrator WTO trade agreements.
2. To provide a forum for trade negotiations.
3. To handle trade disputes.
4. To monitor national trade policies.
5. To provide technical assistance and training for LDCs.
6. To cooperate with other international organizations.

India and the WTO

India was a founding member of the GATT. It actively participated in the Uruguay Round of Negotiations. India strongly favours the multilateral approach to trade relations and grants MFN (most favoured nation) treatment to all its trading partners, including some who are not members of WTO. India has participated actively in all the Ministerial Conferences held under WTO auspices. India is committed to ensure that the sectors in which the LDCs enjoy a comparative advantage are adequately opened up to international trade, and also that the special and differential treatment provisions for LDCs under the different WTO Agreements are translated into specific enforceable dispensations, in order that LDCs are facilitated in their developmental efforts. India feels that the multilateral system would itself gain if it adequately reflected these concerns of the LDCs, so as to create the necessary impetus to enable developing country members to catch up with their developed country counterparts.

Fifth Trade Policy Review (TPR) of India

In order to promote transparency and provide better understanding of the trade policies and practices of its Members, the World Trade Organization (WTO) has a mechanism for regular review of their trade policies. TPR provides the country under review a feedback on its performance in the WTO system. For this purpose, the WTO Secretariat prepares a detailed report on the trade policies and practices of the country under review (Secretariat Report), which is supplemented by a policy statement of the Government under review (Government Report). These two reports form the basis for the review, and are public documents, available on WTO website.

The TPR offers opportunity to other WTO Members to ask questions and raise concerns on different aspects of policies and practices of the country under review. These written advance questions, generally based on the contents of the Secretariat Report and the Government Report, are required to be replied in writing by start of the review meeting.

Depending upon its share in world trade, each Member's trade policy is reviewed by the WTO at fixed periodic intervals. India's Trade Policy Review is carried out every 4 years.

The Fifth TPR of India was held on September 14 and 16, 2011 at WTO, Geneva. Before the meeting, the WTO Secretariat circulated a compilation of India's written replies to 886 advance questions raised by 26 WTO members. Replying to these questions required co ordination involving almost 70 Departments and Ministries of the Government of India.

On September 14, 2011, the proceedings started with the introductory remarks of the chairperson of the TPRB (Trade Policy Review Body). This was followed by the opening statement of the Commerce Secretary, who led the Indian delegation, giving an overview of policies and new developments. Thereafter, the discussants spoke on main issues covered in the WTO Secretariat Report and the Government Report. The subsequent proceedings witnessed oral interventions from 42 WTO Members.

During the review, most of the members commended the resilience of Indian economy that smoothly withstood the adverse effects of global financial crisis without taking recourse to protectionist measures. Members appreciated India for using its trade policy to promote sustainable development and inclusive growth. Members also noted India's positive engagement in Doha Round negotiations. Some of the Members, notably US, raised concerns in certain areas, viz. tariffs and duties; licensing and restrictions; trade defence measures (anti-dumping), government procurement, incentives schemes to promote investments and exports, tariff protection on agriculture, services and investments.

Following responses to the issues raised were provided in India's closing statement on September 16, 2011.

Openness of India's Trading Regime: Questions were asked about the openness of India's trading regime. In response, India pointed out that year after year, India's imports had outpaced exports. In terms of percentage of GDP, the country's merchandise trade deficit is one of the highest in the world. India has been autonomously reducing its tariffs over the years. The simple average most favoured nation (MFN) tariff rate declined from 15.1 percent in 2006-07 to 12 percent in 2010-11. The tariffs on 71 percent of India's tariff lines are between 5 and 10 percent.

Gap between India's Bound and Applied Rates on Agricultural Products: Some members mentioned the large gap between India's bound and applied rates on agricultural products. India responded that the large gap reflected India's steady and continued autonomous tariff liberalization. During the 4 years since the last TPR, the tariffs on some agricultural commodities had to be adjusted in the face of high volatility in food prices. In most cases, tariffs have been brought down and have stayed down. In a few instances they have been raised again but never above their original levels.

Export Incentives: Questions were asked about export promotion schemes. It was explained that India's export promotion schemes are based on the concept of duty neutralization and providing a level playing field. These schemes are reviewed regularly.

FDI Policy: To a number of questions on FDI policy, India explained that the continuing thrust, during the period since India's last TPR in 2007, has been on making the FDI policy more liberal and investment-friendly. The FDI guidelines have been significantly rationalized, simplified, and consolidated, with the aim of providing a single policy platform for reference of foreign investors. Several new sectors such as petroleum and natural gas and civil aviation were either opened up to foreign investment or significantly liberalized during this period. Efforts were also being made to streamline and simplify the business environment and make regulations conducive to business.

Intellectual Property (IP) Policies and Enforcement: On questions related to India's IP policies, India replied that a number of initiatives have been taken to enhance IP protection and enforcement. The changes proposed in the Copyright and Trademark Acts would enhance protection to intellectual property rights (IPRs) in digital technology, particularly with regard to the dissemination of protected material over digital networks. These have been supplemented by administrative as well as judicial measures to strengthen the IPR regime. The provisions on IP protection in these laws are further supplemented by border measures to prevent the import of goods involving copyright piracy and counterfeit trademarks. Another initiative taken by Indian customs is the facility for online registration by the right holders through the web based Automatic Recordation and Targeting for IPR Protection System.

Government Procurement: On this subject, India explained that the procurement of high tech items and high value tenders, above US$ 50,000, is generally open to international bidders. Major reforms are on the anvil for increasing coverage, improving transparency and efficiency, and better enforcement, which are triggered by domestic concerns relating to enhancing the value for money. An omnibus procurement law applicable to the entire country and to all procuring entities, including public sector enterprises, is being deliberated upon.

Sanitary and Phyto-sanitary (SPS) and Technical Barriers to Trade (TBT) Measures: In response to question on SPS and TBT measures, India explained that specific trade concerns raised against India have been largely addressed. Regulations adopted in the past have been on the basis of scientific risk analysis.

Export Restrictions: There were some questions on India's use of export restrictions. India responded that export restrictions have been used on some occasions for purposes of domestic supply management but these have been purely on a temporary basis. The ban on the export of rice and wheat had to be extended in 2009 due to a dislocation in production and again in 2010 due to the severest drought in the country in the last 40 years. However, the export of wheat and non-basmati rice is now completely free. The export of basmati rice is and has always been free. Restrictions on cotton exports were imposed for only a brief period last year. Cotton yarn exports have been made completely free. Similarly, cotton is also freely exportable.

Other Issues: There were questions related to customs valuation, tariffs, and other charges, internal taxation, import licensing, and the use of trade remedies. In response, it was pointed out that India cannot be accused of protectionist intent in its use of trade remedies. If that were the case, then the easy route of increasing the tariffs up to the bound rates could have been used; that has not been done. Anti-dumping measures are legitimate instruments against unfair trade practices.

Investigations are carried out in a fair and transparent manner and subjected to strict scrutiny. As a rule, India only imposes the lesser duty and not the full dumping margin as is done by some WTO members. This underscores the fact that trade remedies are not used as a protectionist tool.

Despite the fact that many members, with very deep pockets, use subsidies as part of their trade policy, India has not imposed a single anti-subsidy measure. As on date, there is only one safeguard duty in force. In the wake of the economic crisis, there was a spurt in application of safeguard investigations in 2009. A total of 14 applications were received but in 9 cases, investigations were either terminated or a decision was taken not to impose any safeguard duty. Duties were imposed only in 5 cases and those too have since been withdrawn. Moreover, India has never taken recourse to quantitative restrictions as safeguard measures. Import licensing affects only a few restricted items primarily on grounds of protection of human, animal, and plant life and the environment. The licensing regime is open and transparent. Licences are granted on a non-discriminatory basis. The relevant regulations are all available in the public domain and the Director General of Foreign Trade (DGFT) acts as the nodal agency.

Recent WTO Negotiations and India

The Doha Round of trade negotiations in the WTO made very little progress after 2008. Throughout 2009 and 2010, discussions continued but no headway was made on any substantive issue in the negotiations. However, the subject featured on the agenda of almost every major international meeting and there were strong affirmations of political support for an early conclusion of the Doha Round. Discussions continued in Geneva during March and April 2011, in a variety of formats. Reports on each area of the negotiations were issued on April 21, 2011. These documents provided an overview of the status of negotiations in each area covered in the Doha Development Agenda.

The focus then shifted to the possibility of selecting some issues for finalization as an *early harvest* in time for the Eighth Ministerial Conference of the WTO in December 2011. It began with an attempt to select issues of particular importance to least developed countries (LDCs). However, these attempts did not meet with any success and proved not only unproductive but very divisive as well. Members could not agree on the issues to be included and sought to selectively bring in various issues of commercial interest to them. Gradually, as Members brought in non-LDC issues, the discussion veered away from the LDC issues. The LDC issues included: (a) duty free quota free (DFQF) market access, (b) rules of origin for DFQF market access, (c) LDC waiver in services, and (d) issues relating to cotton (domestic and export subsidies for cotton and tariffs).

Eighth Ministerial Conference, Geneva, December 2011: In October-November 2011, concerted efforts were made by some of the developed country members of the WTO to use the G-20 Leaders Summit in November 2011 to advance an agenda for the Eighth WTO Ministerial Conference scheduled to be held in Geneva in December 2011. Specifically, they wanted to set the stage for plurilateral agreements on selected issues in the WTO negotiations (rather than multilateral agreements); get WTO members to agree to a commitment abjuring the use of export restrictions; and introduce new issues for negotiation, namely climate change, energy security, and food security.

The weeks preceding the Eighth WTO Ministerial Conference saw hectic activity in the WTO as some members attempted to put various issues on the agenda for ministerial decision. These proposals, however, did not receive support amongst WTO members. At the Eighth Ministerial Conference from December 15 to 17, 2011, ministers adopted a number of decisions on intellectual property (IP), electronic commerce, small economies, LDCs' accession, a services waiver for LDCs, and trade policy reviews. A number of members expressed strong reservations about plurilateral approaches. Many members stressed that any different approaches in the work ahead should conform to the Doha mandate, respect the single undertaking, and be truly multilateral, transparent, and inclusive.

In looking at future work, a large number of ministers

stressed the centrality of development. Many underlined the need to give priority to issues of interest to LDCs, including cotton. Many mentioned the importance of all three pillars in the agriculture negotiations. Many also mentioned trade facilitation, special and differential (S&D) treatment, S&D monitoring mechanism and NTMs. In an unprecedented display of unity, a coalition of more than a hundred developing countries, including India, Brazil, China, and South Africa, met on the sidelines of the Conference and issued a declaration emphasizing the development agenda.

Ninth Ministerial Conference, Bali, December 2013: The Ninth Ministerial Conference of the WTO held in Bali, Indonesia in December 2013 strengthened the credibility of the WTO as an institution. It reaffirmed India's leadership role amongst the developing countries and demonstrated its constructive approach in negotiations. It was made amply clear that while being fully prepared to engage, India will never compromise on fundamental issues pertaining to food security, livelihood security, and the welfare of its poor.

An important development in Bali was the countries entering into trade facilitation (TF) agreement. India's persistent efforts, along with those of other like-minded countries, eventually resulted in either elimination of unwarranted parts of the negotiating text or suitable modifications therein to resolve implementation difficulties. India's consistent position in the WTO has been that matters pertaining to livelihood, food security, and rural development are of vital importance. It was made clear that without a satisfactory decision on food security, India considered the Bali Package as lacking in horizontal balance and would, therefore, not be able to support it. The outcome on the food security proposal provides an opportunity to begin correcting some of the imbalances in the trade rules which are part of the historical legacy of imbalance in the WTO.

One of the elements of the Hong Kong Ministerial Declaration of December 2005 was to extend duty free quota free (DFQF) access to the LDCs. The Ministerial decision taken at the Ministerial Conference in Bali in December 2013 on this issue stated that countries that have not provided such access for at least 97 percent of products 'shall seek to' improve the number of products covered. India became the first developing country to extend this facility to LDCs when it announced a duty free tariff preference (DFTP) scheme for LDCs in 2008. Effective from 1 April 2014, the DFTP Scheme will provide duty-free market access on 96.4 percent of India's tariff lines and 2 percent of the lines would be enjoying preferential duties.

14

Globalization and India

Introduction

A firm commitment to democracy, advances in technology, health, education and the economy, teamed with a new mindset is helping India make its mark in the global arena in a big way. What has probably changed, more than anything else, is the attitude. Indians are demanding their place in the sun. They refuse to be dismissed as citizens of just another "developing nation", an epithet used for all countries that do not match up to Western standards of development. In fact more than what the government has achieved, Indians have pushed the country way up in the global arena. India is being talked about as the next Asian superpower, along with China. Illiteracy, population, and poverty still haunt Indians, but there are areas in which the country is definitely shining. India's growth rate and its achievements may be far greater, because it is accompanied by a healthy democratic system. In fact, literacy rates have moved up almost 65 percent in 2011, from a meagre 48 percent, a decade back. Our higher education system is lauded across the world. Indians are considered "big players" in software development. A self-confident resurgent India is embracing its role as an Asian superpower.

Technology has touched more lives than we can imagine. Farmers in Punjab, to matchmakers in Mumbai, everyone uses internet, to check everything from weather reports to appropriate alliances. India's national highways are getting even better using the latest technologies. More than economics, what has changed is Indians' confidence in themselves. Indians are no longer apologetic about working hard and making money.

Affluence and money are no longer looked down upon—why we even have celebrity Chefs! Several young people prefer to turn entrepreneurs, than depend on jobs that are hard to come by.

Globalization gained momentum from the mid-1990s. The globalization of markets and marketization of economics, politics and culture was spearheaded by global capitalism. In terms of politics and international relations, globalization means a greater bonding or coming together of nation states. With the collapse of communism, and the end of the Cold War, the fading away of non-alignment and of the North-South conflict, nations are moving closer to each other.

Greater internationalization, globalization and integration seem to be the new order of the day. Regional integration is taking place all over the world. In Europe, the EEC or the European Economic Community has given place to the EU or European Union, where the twenty eight members, despite recent problems, have made further efforts at monetary and financial integration with the ultimate goal of full political union. The erstwhile Soviet Union in its new incarnation as the Russian Federation, and the newly liberated Eastern European countries has joined their former foes of NATO to form a "Partnership for Peace".

In Asia, greater steps towards regional integration have resulted in the formation of AFTA (ASEAN Free Trade Area), while new Pan Asia-Pacific organizations like APEC (Asia Pacific Economic Community) and the EAS (East Asian Summit) have emerged. In North America, the US, Mexico and Canada have rejuvenated the NAFTA (North American Free Trade Area) while in Africa, a fully democratized South Africa, has joined its former frontline enemies in Southern Africa to revitalize the newly named SADC (Southern African Development Community).

In Western Europe, the Mercantilist State was openly interventionist—its goal was not the maximization of welfare, but the increase of State power as well. International trade was an extension of domestic trade, and as an adjunct to its capacity to wage war. Exports were encouraged, imports curbed and gold thus obtained was used as settlement to finance a professional army and navy. The market regulated itself, and the State had minimalist functions in the post industrial revolution.

Socialist economies redefined the goals of the State, from Statism to Capitalism. A "Statist" economic system is one oriented towards maximizing state power, while in a capitalist system maximizing profit is the prime objective. The Soviet Union proved to be a classic case of a Statist economy.

In Statist economies, every major interaction between economic agents is mediated to a greater or lesser extent by the State. This makes decision-making lines run vertically instead of horizontally. This is the opposite of a competitive economy, where to ensure maximum speed and flexibility in decision-making, the lines of interaction run horizontally between consumers, intermediaries, and producers, with no interference from the State.

This shift from statist to competitive economies requires:

1. Reduction in the role and functions of the state.
2. Enforcement of a complex framework of rules and regulations to ensure smooth functioning of the market.
3. Enlargement of state functions and therefore its administrative capacity.
4. Synchronization of withdrawal from direct intervention and the development of regulatory functions for a smooth transition.

The benefits of a globalized economy are as under:

1. Death of distance.
2. Services revolution.
3. Mobility of capital.
4. Price reduction.
5. Expanding markets.
6. New ideas for unexploited areas.
7. Benefits of improved infrastructure.
8. Entrepreneurial efforts towards infrastructure improvement extending a great deal of benefits to consumers like high-

speed telecom lines, internet gateways, global short messaging, and innovative services like WAP (wireless application services).

9. Generation of new ideas to be implemented the world over.
10. Outsourcing of business worldwide and back-office operations.

Globalization should be accepted as an emerging and powerful global reality, which has its own momentum and we as an independent nation should maximize the advantage for our country, and minimize the risks.

Transforming Economies

The transformation from a planned to a market economy does not involve a weakening or withdrawal of the State. On the contrary, it requires a strong state—a state with unquestioned authority to promulgate new laws and considerably enhanced administrative powers to enforce and regulate them.

After a period of glasnost and perestroika, the FSU (Former Soviet Union) adopted "shock therapy" in 1992, dismantling centrally directed and planned production. China on the other hand did not follow and ask for IMF/IBRD help. It kept in place central planning and distribution, and only gradually reduced central intervention.

The shift from plan to market without proper institutions in a market-driven world, only weaken the state. China's economic liberalization has reduced the state's share of the output of its *socialist domain*, without being able to tax the newer sectors of the economy. This has resulted in falling revenue to GDP ratios.

Although India has been the slowest in its reforms, and had the fewest structural problems to cope with, the reforms have reduced the tax to GDP ratios only marginally. The State's role has been weakened, as it has been unable to control expenditure—either of its own or those of the state Governments. Rising fiscal deficits is a major concern for India today.

Liberalization will definitely lead to higher growth in India, and this will bring more resources for the state through greater taxes and duties. If the Government utilises its resources effectively, it can bring dramatic improvements in the lives of common people. Once the Government gets out of the negative job of running and controlling economic activity, and puts its best people in implementing social action and infrastructure, only then will it enhance the quality of life of the worst-off members in society. This is a quiet triumph of democratic capitalism, and it is in the nature of institutions that they are run by modest men.

"The real debate on globalization is ultimately not about efficiency of markets, nor about importance of modern technology. The debate is on "severe asymmetries of power", for which there is much less tolerance now than in the world that emerged at the end of World War II"—*Amartaya Sen*.

"In the home of the brave, land of the free! I will not be put down by a bourgeoisie" says an old American protest song. There may or may not be significantly more inequality today, but what is absolutely clear is that people are far less willing to accept massive inequalities now than they were in 1944, when the Breton Woods agreement led to the establishment of the IMF and World Bank. However, Globalization should not mean we end up as a "frog in the well, whose view of the world is confined to that space".

Managing Different Aspects of Globalization

Foreign Trade and Investment: Our global trade pattern since 1991 is more or less in consonance with political and economic developments the world over. Exports to GCA (general currency areas) have increased. With the collapse of the Soviet Union and the growing turmoil in the newly liberated economies of Eastern Europe, both our exports and imports to and from this region have drastically declined. As a result foreign trade in Rupee terms has virtually disappeared. One favourable aspect of this development is that we now earn more hard currency. Besides we have been obliged to improve the quality of our products greatly. While we should strengthen our position in the US and Western Europe, it is now high time for Indian business to fan out to new regions of the world. In Southeast Asia, Malaysia and Singapore are becoming saturated with Indian ventures and hence we should make further inroads into Indonesia, the Philippines and the Indo-Chinese countries.

In Africa, the Francophone West African countries have been almost ignored; though there does exist scope for an Indian commercial presence. South America and the Caribbean countries can also be explored for Indian expertise and managerial contributions particularly in regard to small-scale industries. Similarly, there are good prospects once Russia opens up Siberia for international ventures. Newly democratized Eastern Europe countries, now part of the EU, offers immense possibilities for our private sector companies to establish production-sharing arrangements. The Government of India has identified many export thrust areas where Indian products should do well, such as marine products, horticulture, floriculture, jewellery, bicycles and granite. Export units in these areas are being provided infrastructural support and development assistance to increase their existing strengths.

It is important to concentrate on a few products where we have a competitive advantage rather than try to make market inroads with an amorphous group of products. It has to be kept in mind that in the new EU (European Union) there will be an increasing demand for "branded goods" with appeal to specific categories of consumers. At the same time, customers around the world will look for products with special fashion appeal. Thus, "niche marketing" will become increasingly important. India has the potential to carve out exclusive "niches" for itself in leather garments for up-market consumers in Europe and in designer cotton wear for the younger generation in the US and Western Europe. Food processing and computer software are also areas which hold a lot of promise for India's overseas business forays.

Right Selection of Personnel: Besides, the product profile and country spectrum, an important aspect in globalization efforts is manpower training. The selection of personnel to go abroad should be very carefully done. Only the best managers who have worked competently in various functional areas at home should be sent abroad. The mindset of people sent abroad should be such that they are equally competent to work in an alien milieu. Thus, a common complaint among Japanese and South Korean business undertakings is that Indian businessmen are overbearing in their dealings and have a supercilious attitude. It has to be realised that while keeping *pace with the West may be important, the grace of the East has to be given due consideration if we want to succeed in East Asia.* This requires proper orientation and cross-cultural training prior to an overseas assignment. The manager working abroad has to deal with people with different value systems, inter-personal behaviour patterns and work practices. He has to interact with such business associates in a culturally appropriate manner. This calls for adequate orientation and training in languages, legal procedures, and customs and above all in suitable reactions and responses so that the sensitivities of the host are always respected.

Monitoring and Feedback: A major weakness in our globalization strategies is improper monitoring and inadequate feedback. Our diplomatic missions through the commercial attaches should take greater interest in our foreign business presence. They should constantly give feedback to the Government of India on the progress of business ventures so that appropriate policy redirections can be attempted. "Country Risk Analysis" should be an integral part of the international business divisions of companies. A global checklist of the performance of enterprises in various regions of the world should be made, so that lessons can be learnt from both successes and failures. A coordinated country-specific policy evaluation of both private and public sector overseas ventures should be undertaken by the Commerce Ministry in style of the celebrated Japanese MITI (Ministry of International Trade and Industry).

This synergetic networking of expertise can be immensely useful in strengthening our globalization efforts. India also has several overseas joint ventures, which promote not only trade but also investment-based economic cooperation. These joint ventures are in diverse fields and in many countries particularly in West Asia and Southeast Asia. Along with these joint ventures, collaborations in the form of consultancies transfer of know-how and management skills have acquired new dimensions. Indian ventures have made efforts to adapt first world technology to the needs of the third world and to impart management know-how in diverse fields including power generation, construction of civil projects, railway operation and other technical services. Such consultancies have been successful in Africa and West Asia. They need to be considerably expanded and strengthened.

India's Approach to Globalization

Globalization involves both interdependence and integration with the rest of the world. Globalization is an attempt by India to join the industrialized and free market economies of the world. It involves discarding the traditional approaches to managing the economy and a massive social and economic experiment with little parallels in history. The "strategic intent" of India must be to become one of the three largest economies of the world. Accomplishing the "strategic intent" of joining a select group of leading economies calls for effective leadership, political will and a shared national agenda. It must be remembered that India has several advantages:

1. A stable and vibrant democracy.
2. Wide use of the English language
3. Availability of world class scientific, technical, managerial and professional manpower.

4. Established Western style corporate democracy and a functioning legal system for grievance redressal and contract enforcement.
5. A growing and sizable middle-class estimated at 300 million.

India should effectively capitalize on these advantages in its quest to globalize. India's experiment with hybrid markets—not centrally planned or subject to market mechanisms may create structural impediments to change. India can rapidly build on its private sector capabilities, and public sector physical infrastructure. However, transition to a market economy will demand that processes that distorted market forces during the last thirty-five years—"the licence-quota Raj"—be eliminated. The recent developments against globalization in Geneva, Seattle, Washington, Prague or Davos have proved that there is an alliance between ultra leftist as well as ultra rightist militants with narrow nationalist outlooks. Indian farmers were joined by Swiss farmers having opposite interests at the recent WTO meetings in Geneva.

It should, however, be kept in mind that the former should benefit from liberalization of agricultural trade, unlike the latter who, with the Japanese are the most protected farmers in the world. It should also be noted that foreign investors and MNCs are not waiting to rush into India, but they have to be assiduously courted, as there is worldwide competition for foreign capital. MNCs no longer represent the demonic face of capitalism today. Massive public funds are needed for much better operations and maintenance expenditure in the power and transport sectors. The miserable conditions of power supply all over India, or deteriorating network of roads require massive public investments which cannot be achieved by domestic investment alone.

Globalization is not solely responsible for the poverty, still prevailing in the LDCs. In India, one hears complaints of the lack of a 'human face' to economic reforms. In "Green Revolution" villages, poverty is retreating and reforms favour the overall movement of the economy. In sluggish areas, reforms are hardly felt and conditions of the poor hardly change. The 'roots' of poverty have little to do with globalization and reforms. Questions have to be asked to local politicians about the failure of 'reforms' in their States. The plains of Bihar could again be the granaries of India as they were with Bengal for a few thousand years till the end of the nineteenth century if proper policies are enforced. In the past ten years, India has been removing barriers to trade, FDI and foreign financial investment. The open market-guided economy has been far more efficient than the command economy. The economy has being growing at a steady growth rate of over 7 percent, experiencing only moderate inflation, and taken all kinds of shocks—the East Asian and American and European meltdown in its stride

Globalization should be accepted as an emerging and powerful global reality, which has its own momentum and we as an independent nation should maximize the advantage for our country, and minimize the risks.

The transition from a closed to a vibrant economy will take time and will not be painless. It requires much greater agility and less tolerance of waste and sloth. We have too much tolerance of waste, non-work and survival of the inefficient and self-seeking today in India than other fast growing countries.

Obstacles to globalization and increased FDI are:

- Ground level hassles.
- Obstructionist regulatory framework.
- Rigid and inflexible tax and labour laws.
- Inadequate basic infrastructural amenities like transport power and water.

The suspicions about multilateral organizations like WTO, IBRD, and IMF are ill-founded. Multilateral fora and global rules give more of a chance to the weak than bilateral engagement does.

Easier travel and links are helping Indian standards and

quality approach at international levels. Standards include soft organizational aspects such as reliability and professionalism. Improving standards will allow us to benefit from our lower costs and help us to increase our share in global trade.

Globalization has become a metaphor for the conditioning framework, which shapes and standardizes our choices. It entrenches corporate values at the epicentre of our society, and it does this through the international and national structures, which facilitate the mobility of capital and speculative finance. Globalization provides a view of the world in which the interests of the powerful are defined as necessity, while the demands of the poor appear as greed, which undermines economic success.

The ideology that underpins globalization focuses on trade as the vehicle for improving the conditions of people everywhere. It is an old idea, which sees the increasing integration of international economies as a positive step and one, which would inevitably occur, if governments did not unduly hamper markets. The restructuring associated with globalization doesn't even attempt to promise anything to those traditionally disadvantaged in our society—the unemployed cannot expect jobs, the poor cannot expect prosperity, and women and other disadvantaged people cannot expect equality.

India has achieved considerable constitutional success in reconciling varied regional, caste, and linguistic diversities. She is a triumph of multiculturalism with 29 States and 9 Union territories, held together under exceptionally difficult circumstances. Ultimately democracy is the only way out for the world. The rise of neo-European fascism and neo-Nazism is doomed to failure. The forces of liberalization and globalization will bind together, with appropriate safety nets. India is a "non-territorial cultural nation"—it has always been so. It can never be "conquered" in that sense. India never needed a "functional" State—"A State of India"—governing all of it. The "roots of India" draw their sustenance directly from the nutrition provided by Indian society.

Conclusions

The reform agenda for the future should be:

- Reform rigid labour laws, but take into account the genuine concerns of labour.
- Revitalize agriculture—if necessary a second "Green Revolution". The present agricultural growth rate of 2 percent should increase to at least 4 percent.
- Drastically strengthen rural infrastructure, but also overhaul existing infrastructure.
- Reduce fiscal deficit to manageable limits, and factor in monetization of fiscal deficits in future scenarios.
- Privatize urban infrastructure—but also redeploy and retrain displaced labour in a satisfactory manner.
- Reform the delivery effectiveness of primary education and health care. The schemes in which government still has an important role.
- To achieve increasing success in the knowledge-economy of tomorrow-KPO (knowledge process outsourcing) needs serious country-risk analysis.
- Strengthen and open new channels of employment outside the IT-ITES world.
- The risks of the global economy need to be seriously researched and integrated into the "reform" agenda. Crude price increase, threats to global peace and security, evolving neighbourhood scenarios, SAARC, ASEAN, WTO, have to be well documented.

India will continue down the relatively disorderly path of participatory democracy, raucous, contention prone, often exasperatingly slow and somewhat tardy compared to the tight hand of totalitarian governance, like in China. India will continue to accommodate and absorb several contradictions. In India, unlike in China, the individual can command the State, but money cynically is indifferent to such philosophical or ideological esotericism.

India's breathtaking originality and sophistication has something more profound to offer to the world than its ability to imitate America's deeply flawed consumer society.

Indian intellectuals would best serve India's greatness by speaking frankly about the historic tasks and responsibilities that await the country, and disciplining fantasies and delusions lying in her path.

If India can combine its hard and soft powers, it will surely become a "smart power"—it has already passed the test of political participation that China has not. India is also rapidly adapting to a consensual set up that many foreigners find attractive. Despite its flaws, it is a safe bet that India is a "smart power of the future".

To succeed in today's India, one does not need a legacy of wealth or connections. Its knowledge-based competence is on show, not only in information technology, but across a broad spectrum of activities, including the arts. That a nation of more than a billion people, ranging from the super-rich to the abysmally poor, continue to practice what may be the world's most open system of government is nothing less than a miracle. India's greatest achievement is remaining a vibrant democracy, under exceptionally difficult circumstances.

References

Acharya, Shankar "Can India Grow Without Bharat?", Academic Foundation, New Delhi, 2007.

Bhagwati, Jagdish N., "In Defence of Globalization", Oxford University Press, New Delhi, 2007.

Ghosh, Jayati and C.P. Chandrashekhar, "The Market that Failed", Leftword Books, New Delhi, 2004.

Guha, Ramchandra, "India after Gandhi: The History of the World's Largest Democracy", Macmillan, London, 2007.

Guruswamy, Mohan and Ronald Joseph Abraham, "Redefining Poverty: A New Poverty Line for a New India", Centre for Policy Alternatives, New Delhi, 2006.

Jha, Prem Shankar, "The Perilous Road to the Market: The Political Economy of Reform in Russia, India and China", Pluto Press, London, 2002.

Kelly, David, Ramakishan Rajan and Gillian H.L. Goh, "Managing Globalization-Lessons from China and India", World Scientific

Publication Ltd., Singapore, 2006.

Mahbubani, Kishore, "The New Asian Hemisphere: The Irresistible Shift of Global Power to the East", *Public Affairs*, New York, 2008.

Nayyar, Deepak, "Globalization and Development" in Ha-Joon Chang (eds,*)*, Rethinking Development Economics, Anthem Press, London, 2006.

Pranab Bardhan, "Inequality in India and China: Is Globalization to Blame?", Yale Global, 2007.

Sen, Amataya, "Argumentative Indian: Writings on Indian History, Culture and Identity", Penguin Books, New Delhi, 2006.

Singh, Jaswant, "A Call to Honour: In Service of Emergent India", Indiana University Press, Indiana, 2006.

Smith, David, "The Dragon and the Elephant: China, India and the New World Order", Profile Books, London, 2007.

Srinivasan, T.N., "Comments on From "Hindu Growth" to Productivity Surge: The Mystery of the Indian Growth Transition", IMF Staff Papers, September, 2005, Vol. 52, No. 2.

Zakaria, Fareed, "The Post-American World", Allen Lane, London, 2008.

Bibliography

Bibliography

Abrol, D., "The Government Trips", *The Economic Times*, 5th June, 1993.

Acharya, Shankar, "Can India Grow Without Bharat?", Academic Foundation, New Delhi, 2007.

Ahmed, E., "Regional Cooperation in South Asia and India's Role", *ISDA Journal,* New Delhi, 15(3), 1983.

Akrasanee, N. "ASEAN Economic Cooperation", in L.C. Martin, (ed.), The ASEAN Success Story: Social, Economic and Political Dimensions, Honolulu: East West Centre, 1987.

Ali, Alatas, "Clash of Civilizations? No it is Pure Evil", *Straits Times*, 16th July, 2004.

APEC, "Achieving the APEC Vision: Free and Open Trade in the Asia-Pacific", Second Report of the Eminent Persons Group, August, 1994.

APEC, "APEC Economic Leaders' Declaration of Common Resolve", Bogor, Indonesia, November, 1994.

Ariff, M. and N. Hal, "Export-Oriented Industrialisation in Sydney", Allen and Unwin, The ASEAN Experience, 1987.

ASEAN Round Table, "ASEAN Cooperation Agenda for the 1990s", Singapore: Institute for South East Asian Studies, 1987.

"Asian Economic Integration: Vision of a New Asia", Conference Proceedings, RIS, Tokyo, November 2004.

Bajpai, Kanti, "Enhancing Ties between India and South East Asia: An Indian View", in Satu P. Limaye and Ahmed Mukarram (eds.) India Southeast Asia and the United States: New Opportunities and Prospects for Co-operation, *ISEAS,* Singapore 1998.

Balls, Edward, "Divining the Motives for US; Japan Bashing", Financial Times, London, 19th July, 1993.

Baral, L., "SAARC but no 'SHARK' in South Asian Cooperation in Perspective", *Pacific Affairs,* 58(3), 1985.

Bardhan, Pranab, "Inequality in India and China: Is Globalization to Blame?", Yale Global, 2007.

Baru, S., "GATT: Winter of Discontent", *Economic and Political Weekly*, 7th January, 1989.

Barua, Amit, "Renewing Indo-Australian Ties", *Frontline,* 13th May, 2001, 49-50.

Bhagwati, Jagdish N., "In Defence of Globalization", Oxford University Press, New Delhi, 2007.

Bhanoji Rao, V.V., "APEC Perspectives and India", *The Economic Times*, Bombay, 10th October, 1994.

Chang, Gordon G., "The Coming Collapse of China", Random House, New York, 2001.

Chang, Meng Kng, "ASEAN's Institutional Structure and Economic Cooperation", *ASEAN Economic Bulletin*, 6(3), 1990.

Debroy, B., "The Uruguay Round: Status Paper on Issues Relevant to Developing Countries", *Foreign Trade Review*, 26, No. 3, 1991.

Debroy, B., "The Uruguay Round and Dunkel Draft", *The Hindu*, 5th February, 1992.

Dhar, B., "GATT and the New Trade Discipline: Prospects for the Developing Countries", National Working Group on Patent Laws, New Delhi, 1992.

Dobson, Wendy, "APEC Cooperation Amidst Diversity", *ASEAN Economic Bulletin*, Vol. 10, No. 3, 1994.

Elek, Andrew, "APEC Beyond Bogor: An Open Economic Association in the Asia-Pacific Region", *Asian-Pacific Economic Literature*, Vol. 9, No. 1, 1995.

"Foreign Equity Investments in Singapore", Department of Statistics, Singapore.

Frederic, Gare and Amitabh Mattoo (eds.,) India and ASEAN: The Politics of India's Look East Policy, Manohar Publishers, New Delhi, 2001.

Friedman, Thomas, "The World is Flat", Allen Pane, Penguin Books, 2005.

Ganekar, Bhagyashree, "Indo-Korean Cooperation: A Blooming Symbiosis", *The Economic Times*, 26th February, 1996.

Garnaut, R., "Options for Asia-Pacific Trade Liberalisation: A Pacific Free Trade Area in China", in Siow Yue (ed.) APEC: Challenges and Opportunities, ISEAS, Singapore, 1994.

Gaur, S., "ASEAN-India Ties Entering a New Phase", *Business Times*, Singapore, 2004.

Ghosh, Jayati and C.P. Chandrashekhar, "The Market that Failed", Leftword Books, New Delhi, 2004.

Ghosh, Jayati, "Divergent Development Models", *Frontline*, September 9, 2005.

Goh, Chok Tong, "Anchored in Singapore, Connected to the World", Speech at the International Enterprise Forum, Singapore, February 2005.

Gonsalves, Eric (ed.), "Asian Relations", India International Centre, Lancer International, 1991.

Guha, Ramchandra, "India after Gandhi: The History of the World's Largest Democracy", Macmillan, London, 2007.

Guruswamy, Mohan and Ronald Joseph Abraham, "Redefining Poverty: A New Poverty Line for a New India", Centre for Policy Alternatives, New Delhi, 2006.

Guruswamy, Mohan et al., "Will India Catch-up with China?", Centre for Policy Alternatives, New Delhi, 2005.

"India: New Economy, Old Economy", Department of Foreign Affairs and Trade, Commonwealth of Australia, 2001.

"India-Singapore CECA: Information Kit", Ministry of Trade and Industry, Government of Singapore, 2005.

Iyer, Nandini, "India and the Indian Ocean", APH Publishing House, New Delhi, 1985.

Janelle, Bonor, "Australia-India Security Relations: Common Interest or Common Disinterest?", Working Paper, No. 67, New South Wales, Australian Defence Studies Centre, April 2001.

Jayanth, V., "Unrealised Potential of Indo-Australian Trade", *The Hindu*, 28th March, 1996.

Jha, P.K., "Reassessing India's Look East Policy", *World Focus*, Vol. 287, 2003.

Jha, Prem Shankar, "The Perilous Road to the Market: The Political Economy of Reform in Russia, India and China", Pluto Press, London, 2002.

Jhunjhunwala, Bharat, "Singapore FTA: Against Asian Unity?", *Business Line*, New Delhi, 2005.

Jiali, Ma, "Relations between China and India towards 21st Century", ICAPS Conference, Hyderabad, 1996.

Jurgen-Richter, Frank and C.M. Pamela, "Recreating Asia: Visions for a New Century", John Wiley and Sons, 2002.

Kelly, David, Ramakishan Rajan and Gillian H.L. Goh, "Managing Globalization: Lessons from China and India", World Scientific Publication Ltd., Singapore, 2006.

Keyela, B.K., "Dunkel Proposals on the New Patent System: Impact on India", National Working Group on Patent Laws, and New Delhi, 1992.

Khergamvala, F.J., "APEC Steps to Remove Trade Barriers", *The Hindu*, 18th November, 1995.

Kumar, N., "Towards an Asian Economic Community: The Relevance of India", RIS-DP #34/2002.

Liang, Margaret, "Singapore's Trade Policies: Priorities and Options", *ASEAN Economic Bulletin*, Vol. 22, No. 1, 2005.

Mahbubani, Kishore, "The New Asian Hemisphere: The Irresistible Shift of Global Power to the East", *Public Affairs*, New York, 2008.

Malhotra, Inder, "India, APEC, ASEAN and ARF", *The Times of India*, 23rd November, 1994.

McPherson, Kenneth, Pai Panandiker and Marika Vicziamy (eds.), "Australia and India in the Context of the Indian Ocean and APEC Regions", Centre for Policy Research, New Delhi, 2000 (mimeo).

Mehta, Rajesh, "Economic Cooperation between India and Singapore: A Feasibility Study", RIS-DP # 41/2003.

Mishra, P.K., "Towards a Framework of South Asian Regional Cooperation", *Foreign Affairs Reports,* New Delhi, 1982.

Nagarajan, S., "Buddhism in Southeast Asia", Report of the Centre for Studies on Indo-China and South Pacific, Tirupati, 1998.

Naisbitt, John, "Mega Trends Asia", Nicholas Brealey Publishing, London, 1995.

Nayyar, Deepak, "Globalization and Development" in Ha-Joon Chang (eds,*),* Rethinking Development Economics, Anthem Press, London, 2006.

Osius, Ted and Raja C. Mohan, "Enhancing India-ASEAN Connectivity", Centre for Strategic and International Studies, Washington, D.C., 2013.

Palley, Thomas I., "The End of Export-led Growth: Implications for Emerging Countries and the Global Economy", Briefing Paper No. 6, Friedrich Ebert Stiftung, Shanghai, March, 1-8, 2011.

Pani, N., "Should Farmers Reject the Dunkel Draft?", *The Economic Times*, 18th January, 1993.

Panchamukhi, V.R. and Rehman Sobhan (eds.) "Towards an Asian Economic Area", Macmillan, New Delhi, 1995.

Panitchpakdi, Supachai and Mark L. Clifford, "China and the WTO: Changing China, Changing World Trade", John Wiley and Songs (Asia) Ptd Ltd.: Singapore, 2002.

Patel, S.J., "The South and the GATT Negotiations on the Services Sector", Ahmedabad: Sardar Patel Institute of Economic and Social Research, 1992.

Pedroni, P., "Fully Modified OLS for Heterogeneous Co-integrated Panels", in Baltagi, B., C.D. Kao (eds.), Advances in Econometrics, Non-stationary Panels, Panel Co-integration and Dynamic Panels, Elsevier Science, New York, 93-130.

Ponkshe, S., "The Management of Intellectual Property", UBS Publications, Pune, 1991.

Prasad, Eswar S., "Effects of the Financial Crisis on the US-China Economic Relationship", *Cato Journal*, 29(2), 223-235, 2009.

Qureshi, Mahvash Saeed and Guanghua Wan, "Trade Expansion of China and India: Threat or Opportunity?", *The World Economy*, 31(10), 1327-1350, 2008.

Ram, R., "Exports and Economic Growth in Developing Countries: Evidence from Time-series and Cross-section Data", *Economic Development and Cultural Change*, 36(1), 51-72, 1987.

Reza, Sadrel, "Economic Policy Reforms in South Asia and SAARC-APEC Trade Cooperation", *DEVINSA South Asian Reviews and Abstracts*, Vol. 7, No. 6, Marga Institute, Colombo, 1994.

Rodrik, Dani and Arvind Subramanian, "From 'Hindu Growth' to Productivity Surge: The Mystery of the Indian Growth Transition", IMF Working Papers 04/77, International Monetary Fund, 2004.

Roger, Cohen, "The Roar of a New Asia is in the Global Horizon", *International Herald Tribune,* April 2005.

Saighal, Vinod, "Re-structuring South Asian Security", Manas Publications, New Delhi, 2000.

Sarma, A. and P.K. Mehta, "Exploring Indo-ASEAN Economic Partnership in a Globalising World", Bookwell, New Delhi, 2002.

Saywell, T., "Singapore's New India Play", *Far Eastern Economic Review*, Singapore, 2001.

Sen, Amataya, "Argumentative Indian: Writings on Indian History, Culture and Identity", Penguin Books, New Delhi, 2006.

Rahul Sen, M.G. Asher, and R.S. Rajan, "ASEAN-India Economic Relations: Current Status and Future Prospects", *Economic and Political Weekly*, 2004.

Shroff, Minoo R., "China's Remarkable Economic Growth: Some Lessons", Forum of Free Enterprise, Mumbai, 2000.

Singh, Jaswant, "A Call to Honour: In Service of Emergent India", Indiana University Press, Indiana, US, 2006.

Smith, David, "The Dragon and the Elephant: China, India and the New World Order", Profile Books, London, 2007.

Soesatro, Hadi, "Implications of the Post-Cold War Politico-Security Environment on the Pacific Economy" in C. Fred Bergsten and Marcus Noland (ed.), Pacific Dynamism and the International Economic System, Washington DC, 1993.

Srinivasan, T.N., "Comments on From 'Hindu Growth' to Productivity Surge: The Mystery of the Indian Growth Transition", IMF Staff Papers, September, 2005, Vol. 52, No. 2.

Stock, J., and Watson, M., "A Simple Estimator of Co-integrating Vectors in Higher Order Integrated Systems", *Econometrica*, 61, (4), 783-820, 1993.

Stockwin, Harvey, "APEC without India: But All is Not Lost", *The Times of India*, 20th November, 1994.

Sudhir Devare, "India and Southeast Asia: Towards Security Convergence", ISEAS, Singapore and Capital Publishing Company, New Delhi, 2006.

Tam, S.Y. "Can Malaysian Manufacturing Compete with China in WTO?", *Asia-Pacific Development Journal*, 8(2), 2001.

Tang, Sumei, E.A. Selvanathan and S. Selvanathan, "Foreign Direct Investment, Domestic Investment and Economic Growth in China: A Time Series Analysis", *The World Economy*, 31(10), 1292-1309, 2008.

Thorbecke, W., "Investigating the Effect of Exchange Rate Changes on Chinese Processed Exports", *Journal of Japanese and International Economics*, 25(2), 33-46, 2011.

Wadhva, C.D., "Economic Cooperation among Countries of ASEAN and SAARC", Centre for Policy Research, 1988.

Wadhva, C.D., "Geo-Economic Positioning of India's Trade and Allied Relations: Perspectives on India's Experience with Regional Integration" in V.A. Pai Panandiker and Ashis Nandy, Contemporary India, Tata McGraw Hill Publishing Company Ltd., New Delhi.

Weatherbee, Donald E., "International Relations in Southeast Asia: The Struggle for Autonomy", Rowman and Littlefield Publishers, London, 2009.

Wong, J. "ASEAN Experiences in Regional Economic Cooperation", *Asian Development Review,* 3(1) (1985).

Yagama Reddy, "The Saga of Indian Culture in Southeast Asia: Retrospect and Prospect", Report of the Centre for Studies on Indo-China and South Pacific, Tirupati, 1998.

Yasheng Huang and Tarun Khanna, "Can India Overtake China?", *Foreign Policy*, July-August, 2003.

Yoo, Jang Hee, "A Future Perspective of APEC", *Asian Economic Journal*, Vol. 9, No. 1, 1995.

Zakaria, Fareed, "The Post-American World", Allen Lane, London, 2008.

Index

Index